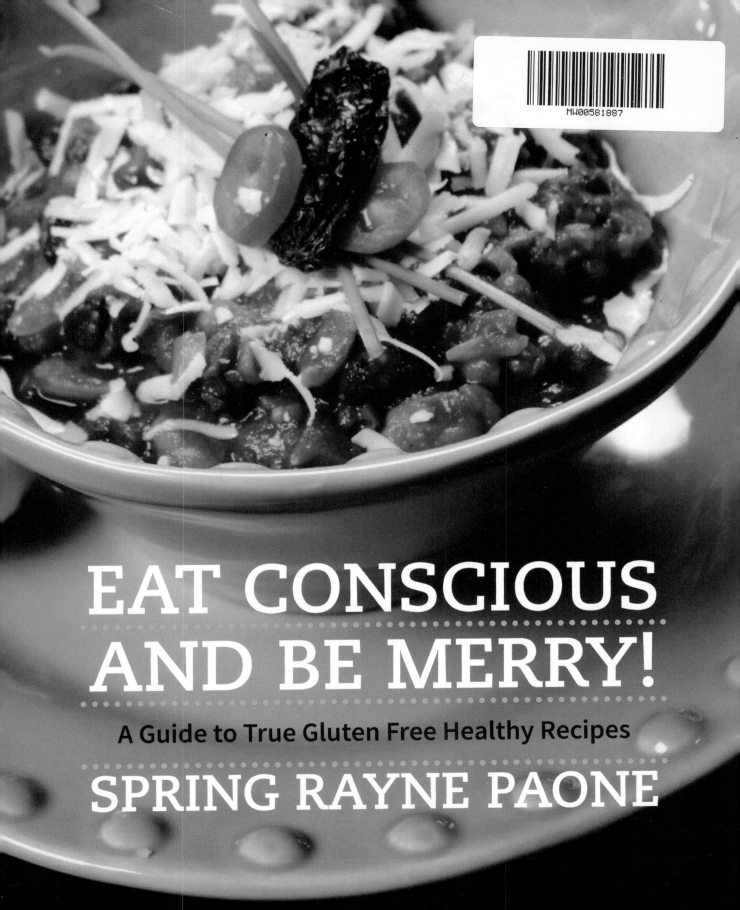

EAT CONSCIOUS AND BE MERRY!

A Guide to True Gluten Free Healthy Recipes

SPRING RAYNE PAONE

Lorrie,

May you Be in Health!

Spring Rayne Paone

Dedication

Two of my dearest friends Elizabeth Gardiepy &
Taerie Gillan are also afflicted with food allergies.
You girls always have my back; I love and thank you
from the bottom of my heart. This book is
for you girls, so we can rise above everything and
ALL Eat Consciously and Be Merry!

Contents

Acknowledgements

I would like to express my thanks and deepest gratitude to my husband Mikey for really going outside the box of his normal carnivore diet. He helped support me and my path by trying everything I made even though he's an extremely picky eater. What a trooper you are - I love you!

I would also like to thank my stepdaughter, Torey Lane Paone, for all the recipe inspirations she has given me. She and I both suffer from major food sensitivities. It was hard to see her little face look at all the donuts & goodies at our huge Italian family gatherings and sometimes cry because the gluten allergy was so unfair. No more tears, honey!

A special thank you to my photography team:

- Meir Kroub - Culinary Photography
- Shay Johnson – Author Headshots & Misc Photos at Maitland Art Center
- Desmond Duquette - Creative Culinary Director

Thank you for supporting me and encouraging me to get this book out.

It certainly takes a village!!

Foreward

Most people's poor eating habits these days are due to boredom, laziness, and fast paced living. Our society has grown away from the nutritious foods we once had at hand to throw something in the microwave and zap it.

A majority of people are not consciously aware of what we are actually putting in our bodies. . Many people that do know don't care and would rather take a pill to "fix it". General Nutrition information is quite vague and there are many hidden truths in our food industry that aren't shared with the public. You really have to dig to find accurate research that isn't monopolized by the Food & Drug Industry.

It has been my lifelong dream to be able to prepare yummy food for people. It gives me even greater pleasure to make food that not only satisfies the taste buds, but is also very nutritious and heals the body.

PART 1

How To
Consciously Eat

How To Consciously Eat

When we become sick, our bodies go into a fight-or-flight mode. It is up to us to pay attention to the signs and what our bodies are trying to tell us. I had various health issues throughout my life which prompted me to learn how to listen to my body, and then to do the utmost research I could on food, nutrition, and various forms of holistic healing. I am proud to say all of my research has paid off. I and many people close to me have been able to overcome various illnesses, such as autoimmune disorders, diabetes, cancers, mental illness, and even weight issues, by following this diet and taking a few herbs along the way. There are so many other things that have been healed, but too many to list. Just by starting to follow these few guidelines and suggestions, you can see a huge difference in less than a week's time.

1. **Throw Out the Microwave!** Why? This device releases severe amounts of radiation into your home environment. It kills any nutrients left in your food after other processing. You then eat that radiation, and no, this doesn't prevent cancer as some of the so-called experts would have you believe. Instead, it *causes* it. Radiation is far more toxic than chemicals or pesticides because it is absorbed at the foods molecular level, not the surface level where chemicals are sprayed. Use a regular stovetop, oven, or toaster-oven instead.

2. **Buy Organic Fruits and Veggies.** Pesticides alone are enough to make us sick and break the body down so we are susceptible to viruses, bacterial infections, etc. There are fourteen pesticides in a strawberry alone! Among these fourteen pesticides, the worst one is Methyl Iodine, which has been proven to cause severe neurological issues, cancers, and miscarriages. If you must buy non-organic fruits and veggies, at least purchase a vegetable wash to help get some

of the surface pesticides off. Unfortunately, washing does not eliminate chemicals that are injected inside for quicker ripening. Some of this occurs before the flowering process but it still not good at all. Support the local organic farmers in your area. If you don't have any, you might consider starting or helping to establish a co-op, and thus make organic produce available to everyone in your area. You can do this by gathering a local group that is interested, and then get a list of the farmers in areas closest to you to see what pricing they can provide. You can go online and look for more information under "building a food or farm co-op."

3. **Learn How to Read Labels.** Seventy-six percent of food manufacturers do not live up to the nutrient information reported on the product labels, according to a US News and World Report in 1990. Imagine how much has changed in the last twenty-one years, especially with so-called "advances" in the farming and cattle industries. Even the USDA Organic Seal label requires that only ninety-five percent, and not one hundred percent, of the product be organic. In fact, they can get away with a product being called "organic" if only seventy percent of it actually is, as long as up to three ingredients on the label are organic. However, such products cannot carry the USDA stamp. Look for products that are one hundred percent organic – you may have a problem finding it locally, but don't give up. Drive a bit farther, or perhaps have products mailed to you (the internet is a great source). Don't accept poorer quality foods if at all possible for the sake of your health and that of your families.

If you have ever experienced food allergies or sensitivities, you can understand how vital it is to read labels on your groceries to know what they contain before putting them into your bodies. Depending on the severity of the allergy or sensitivity, this can become a matter of life and death. Even if you haven't experienced this problem, think of this: have you ever wondered what that ingredient is that's fourteen letters long and pretty near impossible to pronounce? There are so many foods hidden under different names to trick the public into thinking they're getting something better, when in reality, those strange words are simply new names for a harmful chemical.

4. **Cut Out Soft Drinks, Energy Drinks, and Fruit Juices.** They all have high amounts of refined sugar and/or artificial sweeteners that can also lead to cancer and severe malfunctions of the body; especially the liver and pancreas! Yes, artificial sweeteners actually make matters worse for diabetics. Replace these dangerous drinks with mostly water, coconut water, and then green tea, herbal tea and freshly-squeezed vegetable and fruit juices. Juicing is a great habit to incorporate into any diet to maintain health. Juiced veggies may sound disgusting at first, but when you taste the sweet nectar and natural flavors, you will quickly change your mind. Many children actually prefer having a glass of sweet veggie juice over a serving or two of vegetables. I am currently adding more information in a different program that breaks down which fruits, vegetables, and herbs have healing effects on certain ailments in the body.

5. **Become a Vegetarian or Vegan.** Omitting meat alone will increase your health, vitality, length of life and psychic abilities. Meat is FULL of antibiotics, hormones, and animals are treated absolutely horribly. Even hormone-free meat is injected with harmful agents AFTER the animal is slaughtered; they aren't required to give you that information on the package! The misconception and misinformation being promulgated is that people won't get enough iron or protein without eating meat. This is not true at all; you actually get plenty of the right proteins, vitamins and good fats from the veggie and legume diet over the animal diet. That misinformation was brought to you by the FDA and the government-subsidized corporate farm/ranch industry who want the cattle market to grow.

Most people don't know how to do the vegetarian diet properly. I must admit I was lacking a few vitamins and minerals myself, especially since I have so many food sensitivities. The key is to get your levels checked often and ensure you're getting a healthy balance of different foods. Once you do, your body and brain will soar to new heights!

Some people can not find the proper balance to omit the meat. If you have to go back and forth with the meat for awhile, don't consider yourself a failure ever.

You are listening to your body and sometimes you need the meat temporarily until you find the proper balance with foods, herbs and supplements.

The ultimate goal is to stick to only LIVE uncooked food. Even the Bible recommends a vegetarian diet as the original plan for mankind's eating health and habits: "Behold, I have given you every herb-yielding seed which is upon the face of the earth, and every tree, in which is the fruit of a tree yielding seed. To you it shall be for food." (Genesis 1:29)

6. **Start Preparing For The Future of Food.** Things have been shifting on the home garden front. Some areas prohibit vegetable gardens to be visible to other as if they are a big eyesore. Other areas will allow you to garden, but the growing fields are sprayed with aerosol from planes that drop chemtrails from the air almost daily. The soil doesn't have a chance to stay alkaline very long for fruits and vegetables to pollinate properly. These are not the same kind as contrails. Contrails are vapor condensation. Chemtrails are a part of our government's weather modification program. The soils are tested and found to contain high amounts of barium, strontium, aluminum and other toxins. These metals & toxins contribute to many health ailments such as Alzheimer's, breathing conditions, stomach ailments, liver and brain damage. Perhaps you should do some of your own research on this matter. There are a lot of information documentaries on this subject.

A good way to start trying to prepare for the Future of Food is to start learning a thing or two about hydro and aquaponics, solar panels, windmills, compost piles, and rainwater collectors. There are really inexpensive ways to do this and make your own kits. Save your own seeds when you get the organic veggies at the mart. Dry and put them in glass jars labeled for safekeeping in case there is a disaster or famine and we are stuck with no food. Invest in a dehydrator, juicer, vegetable seeds, and alfalfa sprout seeds. Just various sprouts all by themselves have enough nutrients for a whole meal in just one cup.

My favorite gardening is done inside. We have very limited space in my backyard and Florida soil is mostly sand. I use Living Towers Hydroponic System. I even have a grow light so I can grow herbs and veggies all year round. They can be found at www.livingtowers.com.

7. **Know the Dangers of Sugar, High Fructose Corn Syrup (HFCS), Food Dyes and Other Chemicals.** We eat these extremely dangerous foods every day and give them to our children. Sugar alone deteriorates the cells in our bodies. HFCS is chemically-treated sugar highly loaded with mercury. It causes significant weight gain/obesity, cancer, diabetes, bad cholesterol levels, and strongly contributes to severe behavioral problems such as Bi-Polar, Constant irritability, and ADHD. Just avoiding this product alone will help improve your health. Try replacing it with Raw Honey or Raw Blue Agave, or Stevia.

8. **Learn to prepare Raw Foods.** Raw foods are anything that is not cooked over the temperature of 115 degrees. It allows all the enzymes to stay in the food so you get all the proper nutrients your body needs. This book introduces many raw food recipes.

9. **Avoid Gluten!** What is gluten? Gluten is the protein part of wheat, Kamet, spelt, barley, rye, millet, oats and corn. The latest research has even found that the way our rice is processed causes it to contain gluten. NINETY-TWO PERCENT OF THE GLUTEN-FREE DIETS, MENUS, AND PRODUCTS ARE NOT GLUTEN FREE! It's such a shame how everyone is so completely misguided because of the almighty dollar ruling the food and medical industries in America.

Many people like me cannot tolerate gluten when it comes in contact with the small intestine. This is called a gluten allergy. There are tons of people that don't even realize they have this allergy. My grandmother died from it, and I almost did, too. Gluten usually affects every single person in a different way. There are over 300 ailments caused by gluten either directly or indirectly. It is found under numerous hidden names and in so many products you would think to check, such as medication and vitamins, French fries, dry roasted nuts, cosmetics, instant products, sauce mixes, mashed potatoes, dressings, etc. The symptoms include weight gain, weight loss, diarrhea, gas, bloating, abdominal cramps, vitamin and mineral deficiencies, lethargy, brain fog, skin rash, hives, sinus/allergy symptom, muscle and body aches. All symptoms can be minor to severe and hard to pinpoint. I strongly suggest researching more about gluten and what goes into our bodies, especially cross-contamination.

Just following my cookbook, you should be able to transition to the Gluten Free Diet simply and easily.

These are just a few things that could start to help you take a look at food in a new light. This can be really fun if you allow it to be! If you look at it from the point of view that it's difficult, time-consuming, and a futile, that is all you will get out of this journey. I would hope you would choose to find the joy and make the conscious effort to make some changes in your health and that of your families. This diet will help you stay in line with the Universe and to be able to be in the constant flow of NOW! ☺ EAT TO LIVE, LIVE TO EAT AND BE MERRY!

PART 2

The Supplies

The Supplies

Kitchen Supplies – It is very important to have a few of the appropriate kitchen supplies when you are learning to eat gluten-free and tip-toeing into raw foods. Not all of these supplies are necessary; of course, but it will make your life so much easier.

Knives, Choppers, and Blenders vs. Food Processors – Although it's good to gain some muscle by chopping, mixing and gratin your own foods by hand, it certainly is time-consuming. You can either do it by old-fashioned knife, or get a hand chopper. If you use knives, ceramic are preferable because they do not oxidize, and you rarely ever have to sharpen them. If you get your exercise in other forms, and you don't have to do it the hard way, then don't. Take advantage of modern technology if it helps you achieve your goals faster.

You want to at least have a blender, but if you can move up a little, get a food processor with an attachment for slicing and grating. It will speed up your process tenfold. You can also get a 2-speed blender or a big Vita-Mix.

Dehydrator – If you are going to learn these raw food recipes, don't waste your money on a dehydrator that doesn't have a temperature control. That kind only has an on/off switch. You want one that you can control the exact temperature so it doesn't go over one hundred and fifteen degrees. Anything hotter than that destroys the enzymes in your food. At that point, it is no longer considered live, raw food, and you might as well put it in the oven. You can get a dehydrator with several racks, or just a few. I like the bigger one because you have more room to dry or put in a casserole dish if you need to. Small ones work just as well, though.

Juicer – There are several ways to juice your fruits and vegetables. You can do it by hand, of course, with a contraption on which you grind the citrus, but that item doesn't work for other kind of fruit or veggies. What about celery, for instance, or apples? Inexpensive juicers are available at Wal-Mart, but if you purchase one of those, be sure it has a warranty, and make sure you register it. I went through three juicers before I got tired of them breaking down and couldn't have my juice until they'd shipped me a new one. The juicers that have a slower RPM are the way to go. These can juice wheatgrass and other hard-to-juice items, as well as extract more pulp, allowing the enzymes to stay in the juice longer. Juice from a less expensive type must be consumed the same day. Currently, I have the Omega Juicer, which I've used for the past several years without any problems. It come with a pasta extruder and grind grains and nuts into flour.

Baking Pans and Dishes – Since there is so much baking in this book, I do recommend starting a small collection of baking pans. You don't have to go out and buy all new ones at once, just find a recipe you like and go buy the appropriate pan when you shop for the ingredients. Look in local craft stores that have weekly coupons. The pans you will need are: a cookie sheet, bread loaf pan, 9"x13" rectangular pan (metal or glass), 9"x9" square pan, 8"x8" or 9"x9" round pans, muffin pans, donut and /or mini-donut pans, and a tart pan. The baking dishes you will need are: various sized casserole dishes and six personal pot-pie dishes. Of course, you may already own some or all of these, or make do with whatever you have. It's up to your lovely imagination!

Cookware –What we choose to cook our food in make a big difference in our health. Even though non-stick cookware is easy to cook with, it is not the healthiest. It contains C8, which is a likely human carcinogen. If you have any scratched Teflon, please do yourself a favor and throw it out immediately. It can release toxins into the air and of course, your food. A wonderful company, Americraft has a unique product called 360 Cookware. They are an American made and manufactured Green company that has strong family values. 360 Cookware is an energy efficient cooking system that uses Vapor Technology to heat your food quicker and at lower temperatures, thus keeping all the nutrients and the flavors in the meal. I highly suggest this awesome cookware! They can be found at www.americraftcookware.com.

Food Supplies – I realize that most of you haven't heard much about raw foods so some of these will be quite new to you. They were all new to me once, too. It seems living in Florida; we are actually quite behind on the healthy food scene. I used to have to drive at least 30-45 minutes to get to a good health food store that carried everything I need. I am lucky to have a store locally now, as the demand is finally getting a little higher in my home town. I will do my best to explain and introduce new foods so it can be as fun and exciting an adventure for you as it was for me. This change in eating is a major life choice, so why not make it an enjoyable one as well!

Grains and Flours – Since we are doing gluten-free cooking in this book, we must know what grains we can eat. Most grains contain gluten. The ones we can have are generally considered to be in the fruit or vegetable category rather than grain. For instance, buckwheat and quinoa are fruits, and are excellent gluten-free "grains" that aren't really grains at all. Nut flours are a great replacement, but are often dense, rendering a heavier texture when prepared. Each grain has a different kind of gluten protein. Some are considered more harmful to the body than others. I would stick to the ones in this book because they have been tested and retested, and, yes, I was the "guinea pig" so others would benefit from my personal conclusions. Many people who are sensitive or allergic to gluten are generally Blood Type A. If you know anything about the blood-type diet, you know you are not supposed to have dairy, gluten, sugar, alcohol, potatoes, garbanzo bean, meats, various nuts and so many other things. So this book is for people with all those sensitivities. I have found a nice balance of things we can eat, but if you are able to include items outside these restrictions, by all means substitute whatever you can, only try to stay away from the grains regardless.

Tapioca and Arrowroot – Both are a great replacement for corn or potato starch when you need a thickener for gravies or soups. You will find a mixture of these flours help achieve the right consistency in your baked goods.

Xanthan Gum – This is a plant-derived, healthy bacteria gained in the fermentation process. It is used as an emulsifier and helps elasticity in the baked goods.

Cream of Tartar – This is a bicarbonate which is a replacement for cornstarch-based, and thus gluten-laden, baking powder. It is from where the grape wine fermentation creates crystals called Potassium Bitartrate.

Thai Coconuts – These are somewhat sweeter than regular brown coconuts. You don't have to buy organic ones, but it does help. You need to crack them open with a knife and hammer to get the meat, or pulp, out. The coconut water (milk) inside is nature's energy drink, and provides tons of electrolytes for the body.

Cocoa/Cacao – Tomato, tomahto – it's all pretty much the same, but if you are looking for it on labels, Cacao shouldn't be processed. Basically you are looking for alkaline chocolate. Most of our chocolate is processed and creates an acid environment in the body. The raw form of chocolate is healthy and provides mood enhancing agents, as well as being a great source of trace minerals.

Coconut Oil/Butter – These are the same; you will see that I have listings for both. The coconut butter is usually in a more firm state, while the oil is melted. This has so many health benefits, and helps to fight cancer. I use it in everything! Extra-virgin has less of a coconut taste than regular coconut oil. It's up to you to choose which form to use. This product can be rather expensive to purchase in smaller quantities at the retail level. For this reason, I like to get mine in bulk online at:www.mountainroseherbs.com.

Agave Nectar – Agave nectar is the sweet liquid extracted from the Blue Agave Cactus. There are many ways agave is processed. Try to avoid the highly-processed form, since using it will be just as bad as eating sugar. Raw Organic Blue Agave is the best and purest form. While it costs a bit more, it is worth the benefits of putting something that hasn't been processed into your body. Agave is also sweeter than sugar, but does not affect blood-sugar levels. Just make sure you are not getting it in a processed version or it can be just as bad as the Sugar or HFCS.

PART 3
The Recipes

Breads, Crackers and Wraps

PIZZA CRUST

PASTA DOUGH

BANANA BREAD

BASIL COCONUT FLATBREAD WRAPS

BLACK BEAN FLATBREAD CRACKERS

GARLIC CHEESE BREAD

PUMPKIN CRANBERRY BREAD

SANDWICH BREAD

ZUCCHINI BREAD

Pizza Crust

VEGAN

This is such a versatile pizza crust that can be used in a number of different recipes. Be creative and most of all have fun!!!

Makes 2 small pizza crusts or 1 large
16 Servings Prep Time 5 minutes Cook Time 15 minutes

Dry Ingredients	*Wet Ingredients*
1 CUP TAPIOCA FLOUR	1 CUP WATER, ALMOND MILK OR VEGGIE STOCK
½ CUP ARROWROOT FLOUR	
1 ½ CUP QUINOA FLOUR	¼ CUP COCONUT OIL (MELTED)
1 TSP XANTHAN GUM	
1 ½ TSP SEA SALT	
1 TBSP CREAM OF TARTER	
1 ½ TSP BAKING SODA	

Directions

1. Grease bottom of baking pan & Preheat oven to 400.
2. Mix all dry ingredients together.
3. Add liquid, mix well and add coconut oil, blending well.
4. Divide dough in half.
5. Spread evenly in the bottom of baking pan.
6. Bake 10-15 minutes before adding toppings.

Pasta Dough

SUGAR FREE, VEGAN OPTION

This recipe has the option to make it vegan if you choose. The consistency will be a little jelly-like compared to the one using eggs but the taste is still great. You can cut this into any shape pasta. My favorite thing to make with this recipe is Raviolis. You can get a ravioli press or cut your own 2 ½ - 3 inch squares and press by hand. I find the ravioli press much easier. Look for raviolis and other pasta recipes on pages 92-95.

Serves 8 » Prep Time 45 minutes » Cook Time 20 minutes

Dry Ingredients	*Wet Ingredients*
2/3 CUP QUINOA FLOUR	4 LARGE ORGANIC HORMONE FREE EGGS OR 2 TBSP VEGAN EGG REPLACER & ½ CUP WATER
2/3 CUP ARROWROOT FLOUR	
4 TBSP TAPIOCA FLOUR	
1 TSP SEA SALT	
1 ½ TBSP XANTHAN GUM	2 TBSP OLIVE, CANOLA, OR COCONUT OIL
EXTRA QUINOA FLOUR INCASE NEED TO THICKEN DOUGH	EXTRA WATER MAY BE NEEDED TO GET THE CONSISTENCY RIGHT

Directions

1. In a large bowl, combine all dry ingredients.
2. In a separate bowl, either beat the eggs or mix the egg replacer powder and water together. Add oil to wet mixture.
3. Add wet ingredients a small bit at a time to the dry, mixing until you have kneaded it thoroughly by hand.
4. Separate into 2 balls.
5. Boil a medium pot of water.
6. Add flour to Cutting Board, Clean Countertop and Rolling Pin.
7. Taking one ball at a time, either roll out by hand, use pasta maker or pasta press.
8. Cook 12-20 min depending on how thick you made the pasta and how well done you like it.

Banana Bread

VEGAN, SUGAR FREE

Mmmmm…Warm Banana Bread! I am happy to say that this one is not only gluten free, but sugar free and already vegan and tastes great. The key is to bake it on lower heat because agave will burn. Also, rotation helps keep it evenly baked when there are no eggs present. This recipe makes perfect loaf bread or muffins.

12-16 Servings » Prep Time 10 min » Cook Time 55 min max

Dry Ingredients	Wet Ingredients
1 CUP QUINOA FLOUR	1 ½ CUP VERY RIPE BANANAS MASHED
1 CUP TAPIOCA FLOUR	½ CUP COCONUT OIL
2 ¾ TSP BAKING SODA	2/3 CUP PLUS 1 TSP AGAVE
1 TSP XANTHAN GUM	1 TSP GLUTEN FREE VANILLA EXTRACT
1 TSP CREAM OF TARTER	2/3 CUP UNSWEETENED ALMOND MILK
1 TSP SALT	4 TBSP COCONUT OIL
1 TSP CINNAMON	
¼ TSP NUTMEG	

Directions

1. Preheat Oven 325 degrees.
2. Grease bread loaf pan thoroughly or prepare papers for muffin tin.
3. In a medium bowl, combine all dry ingredients.
4. In a small bowl, combine all wet ingredients until smoothly blended.
5. Add wet ingredients to dry, blending well.
6. Spread evenly in loaf pan or divide in muffin pan.
7. For loaf, bake 25 minutes, rotate 180 degrees and bake 20-30 min more. For muffins, bake 20 minutes, rotate and bake 25 min more.

Basil Coconut Flatbread/Wraps

RAW

I fell in love with this wrap when I went to a local raw food restaurant. So it took a couple years to formulate this special recipe because almost every wrap on the market has gluten. Enjoy opening the coconuts and grabbing the sweet nectar inside, a double bonus gold-find. Coconut Water is nature's sports drink! A dehydrator is necessary for this recipe to keep it raw, but it must have a temperature gage. No more than 115 degrees please!

8 Servings » **Prep Time 45 min** » **Dehydrate Time 6-8 hours**

Ingredients

4 CUPS OF RAW THAI COCONUT
1 ½ CUP BASIL CHOPPED
2 CUPS WATER
1 ½ TBSP PSYLLIUM HUSK
3 TBSP RAW BLUE AGAVE
1 TSP SEA SALT

Directions

1. Take an old sharp knife and a hammer and cut the top of coconut in a circle. (It may be easier to pound down in a spot and use the hammer and tap the knife along using force to create circle.
2. Pour out the coconut water; take a shot for yourself and save rest in glass jars.
3. Put all ingredients in a food processor. May have to do in half batches depending on the size of your processor.
4. Wet a spatula and spread thin on to dehydrator tray with nonstick sheet.
5. Dehydrate on 115 degrees for about 6-8 hours, if dry, peel sheet away and put back on dehydrator mesh tray wet side up. Dry another 3-4 hours or until dry but pliable. Too dry will cause them to crack.
6. Store them in the refrigerator.

Black Bean Flat Bread Crackers

VEGAN

These Black Bean Crackers give a whole new meaning to hearty snacks. You can eat them alone and get plenty of fiber and protein, or you can spice it up by dipping them in Raw No Bean Hummus on page 137, Fresh Salsa on page 131, Guacamole on page 135, or using them as flat bread or a side dish for pasta.

10-12 Servings » Prep Time 20 minutes » Cook Time: 45 min

Dry Ingredients	*Wet Ingredients*
½ CUP TAPIOCA FLOUR	2 CUPS BLACK BEANS, EITHER CANNED OR FRESH SOAKED
½ CUP QUINOA FLOUR	
½ TSP BAKING SODA	1/3 CUP OLIVE OIL
½ TSP CREAM OF TARTAR	2/3 CUP WATER
½ TSP SEA SALT	3 CLOVES GARLIC MINCED
2 TSBP FLAX, HEMP OR CHIA SEEDS (GROUND)	¼ CUP ONION CHOPPED

Directions

1. Preheat Oven 350 degrees.
2. Mash Black Beans to a paste.
3. Mix all dry ingredients together well.
4. Add Mashed beans and wet ingredients to dry.
5. Mix well either by hand or mixer.
6. Put wax paper over a cookie sheet and dab a little oil on paper.
7. Spread mixture thin over the wax paper. May need 2 pans depending on your desired thickness.
8. Bake 25-30 Min, check and bake another 10-15 if necessary.
   **Shorter cooking time produces a bread, longer for crackers. If making crackers, then cut in squares or triangles, remove from paper, put back on pan and bake 10-20 min longer.

Garlic Cheese Bread

VEGAN OPTION

I used to go to Red Lobster. I was allergic to seafood from a young age, so I would load up on the yummy garlic cheese bread for my meal. Now that I have chosen a new lifestyle of higher vibration food, this is one recipe that brings back those fun days with a new kick and without the pain in the gut. ☺

12-16 Servings » **Prep Time 10 minutes** » **Cook Time 45 min**

Dry Ingredients	*Wet Ingredients*
¼ CUP QUINOA FLOUR, PLUS A TBSP OR SO FOR DUSTING	1/3 CUP OLIVE OIL
1 CUP TAPIOCA FLOUR	¼ CUP ORGANIC RAW AGAVE SYRUP
1 CUP ARROWROOT FLOUR	2 CUPS SHREDDED CHEDDAR CHEESE OR DAIYA VEGAN CHEESE (OPTION) DIVIDE 1 ½ CUP CHEESE IN DOUGH AND ½ OF CHEESE ON TOP OR ALL CHEESE IN DOUGH
¾ TSP BAKING SODA	
1 ½ TSP CREAM OF TARTER	
1 TSP SEA SALT	
1 ½ TSP XANTHAN GUM	
1 TSBP GARLIC POWDER OR 3-4 FRESH CLOVES MINCED	¼ - ½ CUP OF LIQUID EITHER ALMOND MILK, WATER OR VEGGIE STOCK
2 TSP DRIED SAGE OR CHIVES OR A COUPLE SPRIGS (OPTIONAL)	

Directions

1. Preheat Oven **325** degrees.
2. Mix all dry ingredients together.
3. Add wet ingredients one at a time in order, mixing well after each. Add the liquid, slowly, until dough is sticky.
4. Take spoonfuls and shape into 4-5 inch breadsticks.
5. Dust remaining flour on top, sprinkle remaining cheese on top if desired.
6. Bake 20 minutes rotate pan 180 degrees and bake another 15-20 minutes.

Pumpkin Cranberry Bread

VEGAN OPTION

This traditional bread is perfect for the Holidays, giving we gluten-free eaters an option at family dinners. It does contain sugar but not much at all. You can use the egg replacer instead of the eggs to make it a vegan option.

12-16 Servings » Prep Time 10 minutes » Cook Time 55 minutes

Dry Ingredients

1 CUP QUINOA FLOUR

1 CUP TAPIOCA FLOUR

¾ TSP BAKING SODA

½ TSP CREAM OF TARTAR

2 TSP XANTHAN GUM

1/4 TSP SEA SALT

½ TSP CLOVES

½ TSP CINNAMON

¼ TSP NUTMEG

1 CUP DRIED CRANBERRIES

Wet Ingredients

2 CUPS WATER OR ORGANIC ORANGE JUICE

2 ORGANIC HORMONE FREE EGGS OR 3 TSP EGG REPLACER AND 4 TSBP WATER

½ CUP ORGANIC RAW SUGAR FINELY GROUND

½ CUP UNSWEET ALMOND MILK

1 CUP ORGANIC PUMPKIN PUREE (FRESH OR CANNED)

4 TBSP COCONUT OIL

Directions

1. Preheat Oven 375 degrees.
2. Grease bread loaf pan thoroughly or prepare papers for muffin tin.
3. Boil the 2 Cups of Water or Orange Juice, after boiling turn to med/low heat and add cranberries. Cook approx 5-8 min until cranberries are plump.
4. In a medium bowl, combine all dry ingredients.
5. In a small bowl, combine all wet ingredients until smoothly blended.
6. Add wet ingredients to dry, blending well.
7. Drain Water or Juice, fold cranberries into batter.
8. Spread evenly in loaf pans or divide in muffin pan.
9. For loafs, bake 30-45 minutes. For muffins, bake 20-25 minutes. Check for doneness, if necessary turn and bake another 20-30 minutes.

Sandwich Bread

VEGAN

This bread recipe took awhile for me to perfect because I was going for the best consistency for being vegan. It has a tiny amount of sugar and is the only recipe in the book with yeast. It takes a bit of time, but it is sure worth it. You can use this for daily bread, or top with apple butter, preserves or use it for Stuffing on pages 115-117.

12-16 Servings » Prep Time 60 minutes » Cook Time 50 minutes

Dry Ingredients

1 CUP QUINOA FLOUR

1 CUP BUCKWHEAT FLOUR

1 CUP ALMOND FLOUR

1/2 CUP TAPIOCA FLOUR

1 CUP ARROWROOT FLOUR

2 ½ TSP XANTHAN GUM

2 TSP SALT

2 PACKAGES OF DRIED ACTIVE YEAST

2 TEASPOONS ORGANIC CANE SUGAR

Wet Ingredients

2 - 2 1/4 CUPS WARM WATER FOR YEAST ACTIVATION

1/3 CUP OLIVE OIL

1/3 CUP HONEY OR ORGANIC RAW BLUE AGAVE

Directions

1. Grease bread loaf pan thoroughly & lightly dust with flour.
2. Start with just 2 cups of warm water and sugar in a small bowl, add yeast, stir well, let sit for 8-10 minutes, add honey or agave and oil, mix well with fork.
3. In a large bowl, combine the rest of dry ingredients together.
4. Add wet ingredients to dry, blending out lumps as you pour in the wet mixture. If too thick add up to 1/4 cup water and blend until smooth.
5. Spread evenly in loaf pan bake, cover with dish towel, let rise double size for approx 50-60 min.
6. Preheat Oven, 350 degrees, Bake 50 minutes, check for doneness, bake additional 10-20 minutes. Cool about 10 minutes in the pan then cool on wire rack before slicing.

Zucchini Bread

SUGAR FREE, VEGAN OPTION

Not many kids' fancy zucchini, especially if you tell them it's in bread, but this recipe has a way of being quite delicious either warm or cold and the kids would never know its good for them. Zucchini is one of those veggies that are full of health benefits. It aids digestions, helps to prevent constipation, helps lower blood sugar and blood pressure, lowers cholesterol, is an anti-inflammatory and helps prevent cancer, just to name a few.

12-16 Servings » Prep Time 15 minutes » Cook Time 1 Hour

Dry Ingredients	Wet Ingredients
¾ CUP QUINOA FLOUR	1/3 CUP OLIVE OIL OR MELTED COCONUT OIL
½ CUP TAPIOCA FLOUR	1/3 CUP UNSWEET APPLESAUCE
½ CUP ARROWROOT FLOUR	½ CUP RAW BLUE AGAVE
½ CUP GROUND CHIA, FLAX AND/OR HEMP SEEDS	2 TSP GLUTEN FREE VANILLA EXTRACT
¾ TSP BAKING SODA	1 1/2 CUP SHREDDED ZUCCHINI
1 ½ TSP XANTHAN GUM	2 EGGS BEATEN OR 3 TSP EGG REPLACER & 2/3 CUP WATER
1/4 TSP CREAM OF TARTER	
1 TSP SALT	
1 TSP CINNAMON	

Directions

1. Preheat Oven 350 degrees.
2. Grease bread loaf pan thoroughly & lightly dust with flour.
3. In a medium bowl, combine all dry ingredients together.
4. In a small bowl, combine all wet ingredients until smoothly blended.
5. Add wet ingredients to dry, blending well.
6. Spread evenly in loaf pan bake 45-50 minutes, then cover with foil bake another 20-25 minutes. Check middle for doneness with knife or toothpick.
7. Cool on wire rack 30 minutes or completely before slicing.

Breakfast

❦ ⬩ ❧

PANCAKES

HEARTY CREAM OF BUCKWHEAT

RAW BUCKWHEAT CEREAL

WAFFLES

SWEET CREAM OF BUCKWHEAT

Pancakes

SUGAR FREE, VEGAN

This is a really yummy pancake recipe with no sugar added. As I experimented I found that using fruit juice pulp gives the pancakes the best flavor. If you have the time make the fruit juice first to serve with your pancakes, or make the juice a day or so ahead and refrigerate or freeze the pulp. Serve the pancakes with Organic Raw Blue Agave Syrup, or try the flavored ones they have available like chocolate, hazelnut, and berry flavors.

Makes 14-16 » Prep Time 10 minutes » Cook Time 15 minutes

Dry Ingredients	Wet Ingredients
1 ½ CUPS QUINOA, BUCKWHEAT, ALMOND OR PECAN FLOUR	¾ CUP ALMOND MILK
½ CUP ARROWROOT OR TAPIOCA FLOUR	2/3 CUP ORGANIC RAW BLUE AGAVE
2 ½ TSP BAKING SODA	2/3 CUP UNSWEETENED APPLE SAUCE OR FRUIT JUICE PULP
1TSPCREAM OF TARTAR	½ CUP COCONUT OR CANOLA OIL, PLUS SOME FOR PAN
1 TSP SEA SALT	2 TBSP GLUTEN FREE VANILLA EXTRACT
½ TSP XANTHAN GUM	OPTIONAL – 2/3 CUP MASHED BANANA, BERRIES OR CHOPPED CHOCOLATE OR CAROB CHIPS
1 TSP CINNAMON	

Directions

1. In a medium bowl, combine all dry ingredients.
2. Add wet ingredients to dry, mix well.
3. If you are adding optional mixed fruit or chips, fold it in gently.
4. Heat Pan or griddle on medium heat.
5. Add a small amount of oil to cover the pan.
6. Pour batter in small circles on pan or griddle, cook until you see holes.
7. Flip and continue cooking until done.
8. Top with Organic Raw Blue Agave or Real Maple Syrup.

Hearty Cream of Buckwheat

VEGAN, SUGAR FREE

For those of you who miss Cream of Wheat or Grits this one is for you. Just a small bowl of this buckwheat feeds the body and soul on so many levels. This particular recipe is for those who don't necessarily like sweets in morning. It also makes a wonderful quick snack when you need some energy before preparing a big meal too.

Makes 4 Servings » Prep Time 5 minutes » Cook Time 10 minutes

Ingredients

1 CUPS OF CREAM OF BUCKWHEAT

1TSP SEA SALT

**5 CUPS OF WATER & 4 ½ TSP VEGGIE STOCK CUBES OR POWDER
OR LIQUID VEGGIE STOCK**

3 CLOVES GARLIC MINCED OR 1 TSP GARLIC POWDER

½ CUP ONIONS CHOPPED OR 1 ½ TSP ONION POWDER

Directions

1. Add veggie stock, water and salt to a pot and bring to a boil.
2. While the water is coming to a boil, chop onions and garlic and set aside.
3. Add buckwheat to boiling water, wait for it to boil again, stir well, and turn to lowest heat, adding onions and garlic, stirring frequently.
4. Cook approximately 10 minutes until all water has been absorbed.

Raw Buckwheat Cereal

VEGAN, SUGAR FREE, RAW FOOD

This cereal is quite versatile. It is best served with Raw or Unsweet Original Almond milk or you can snack on them dry like cookies. They store for months if packaged properly and are great for traveling. This is one of my favorite snacks for keeping raw on my road trips. They provide many nutrients and are just sweet enough to enjoy as an after dinner treat without the guilt.

Makes 10-12 Servings » Prep Time 1 ½ hours » Total Time 13 Hours

Dry Ingredients

2 CUPS OF BUCKWHEAT GROATS (SOAKED 1 ½ HOURS)

2 TSP SEA SALT

1 ½ TBSP CINNAMON

¼ CUP DRIED STRAWBERRIES OR BLUEBERRIES(OPTIONAL)

Wet Ingredients

½ CUP ORGANIC PURE MAPLE SYRUP

¼ CUP RAW BLUE AGAVE

Chocolate Variation

EXCHANGE CINNAMON FOR RAW COCOA POWDER OR CAROB

Directions

1. Drain and rinse buckwheat groats very well.
2. Combine all ingredients except berries in food processor, blend well but leave a bit chunky.
3. Pour or drop batter on dehydrator sheets in small circles
4. Dehydrate 115 degrees 10-12 hours. Flip; add berries if adding, then dry 3-4 more hours.

Waffles

VEGAN, SUGAR FREE

These waffles are so delicious, most of my guests have no idea it is gluten-free. Using a gluten free recipe with a waffle iron, these will cook a bit differently. I would put it on a medium setting, pour in your batter, and wait until the timer goes off about 10 minutes. If the middle is still uncooked, then put it in the toaster oven for 5 minutes or since the waffle iron may burn the outside too much.

Makes 8 Belgian or 16 Regular Waffles » Prep Time 15 minutes » Cook Time 15 minutes

Dry Ingredients	*Wet Ingredients*
1 ½ CUPS QUINOA FLOUR	2 ½ CUPS ALMOND MILK
1 CUP TAPIOCA OR ARROWROOT FLOUR	¼ CUP OF COCONUT OIL OR CANOLA AS SUBSTITUTE
1 TSP SEA SALT	1 TBSP GLUTEN FREE VANILLA OR ALMOND EXTRACT OR MIXTURE OF BOTH.
½ TSP BAKING SODA	
1 TSP CREAM OF TARTER	
¾ TSP XANTHAN GUM	

Directions

1. Preheat and lightly grease waffle iron.
2. In a large bowl, combine all dry ingredients.
3. Add wet ingredients one at a time, combining well after each ingredient.
4. Stir all ingredients until smooth.
5. Add a little oil to waffle iron and spoon batter in evenly filling all the holes.
6. Follow waffle iron directions, approximately 10 minutes per waffle batch.
7. If necessary bake another 5-10 minutes in toaster oven.

Sweet Cream of Buckwheat

VEGAN, SUGAR FREE

Growing up in Florida, where the weather is constantly warm and balmy, I rarely ate a hot breakfast. However, during those short few weeks of cooler temperatures, we got to enjoy oatmeal. I came across this by accident one day at the grocery store and thought, FINALLY- my oatmeal replacement!

Makes 4 Servings » Prep Time 5 Minutes » Cook Time 20 minutes

Ingredients

1 CUPS OF CREAM OF BUCKWHEAT

5 CUPS OF WATER, ALMOND MILK OR COCONUT WATER

1 ½ TSP CINNAMON

½ CUP RAISINS OR OTHER DRIED FRUIT

(CRANBERRIES, STRAWBERRIES, BLUEBERRIES, PEACHES

1 TBSP RAW BLUE AGAVE

¼ CHOPPED NUTS (OPTIONAL)

Directions

1. Bring water or milk to a boil
2. Add buckwheat to boiling water, wait for it to boil again, stir well, and turn to lowest heat, stirring frequently.
3. Cook approx 10 minutes until all water has been absorbed.
4. Add fruit, nuts and cinnamon.

Desserts

CARROT CAKE OR DONUTS

BASIC BROWNIES

CHILLAXIN' BROWNIES

PURE ENERGY BROWNIES

CHOCOLATE MOUSSE

KEY LIME TARTS

MACAROON MOUNDS

FROZEN FRUIT SORBETS

FROZEN MOUSSE POPS

RAW FRUIT PIES

STRAWBERRY DONUTS

RED VELVET CAKE

VANILLA CAKE

VANILLA CAKE DONUTS

Carrot Cake or Donuts

SUGAR FREE, VEGAN

You can turn any of the bread or cake recipes into donuts, with or without icing. Kids love that they can have those yummy donuts again. You will need a non-stick donut pan or two. The mini donut ones are fun too, and are just a bit more time consuming to fill. Wilton makes a great inexpensive pan. Use your pulp scraps from making one of the veggie or fruit juices. When you are juicing just keep the carrots scraps separate. Sometimes I throw in a bit of apple if I am short on the carrot pulp. The apple adds a bit of extra sweetness. See Icing Recipe on Page 124.

12-16 Servings » Prep Time 20 minutes » Cook Time 40-50 minutes

Dry Ingredients	Wet Ingredients
1 CUP QUINOA FLOUR	½ CUP CRUSHED WALNUTS OR ALMONDS (OPTIONAL)
1 CUP ARROWROOT FLOUR	
1 CUP TAPIOCA	3 CUPS ORGANIC CARROT PULP FROM JUICE OR SHREDDED CARROTS
1 TBSP BAKING SODA	
2 ½ TSP XANTHAN GUM	
1 ¼ TSP SALT	1 CUP ORGANIC RAW BLUE AGAVE
½ TSP CLOVES	2/3 COCONUT OIL
1 TBSP CINNAMON	1 CUP UNSWEET ALMOND MILK
2 ¼ TSP GINGER	½ CUP HOT WATER
½ TSP NUTMEG	

Directions

1. Preheat Oven 325 degrees.
2. Grease cake or donut pans thoroughly.
3. In a large bowl, combine all dry ingredients.
4. In a medium bowl, combine all wet ingredients except for carrots and water.
5. Add wet ingredients to dry, blending well.
6. Add hot water then fold in carrots, mix well.
7. Spread evenly in cake or donut pans.
8. For cake bake 25 minutes, rotate pan, bake 25 minutes more. For donuts, bake 20 minutes, rotate pan, and bake 20 min more.

Basic Brownies

SUGAR FREE, VEGAN

A girl's weakness is chocolate. It helps to elevate our moods, and make us giddy and happy. This recipe allows you to still enjoy brownies without the guilt of sugar, and its even vegan. On the following pages you will find other wonderful variations of these decedent treats.

Serves 12-16 » Prep Time 10 minutes » Cook Time 20-30 minutes

Dry Ingredients	*Wet Ingredients*
3/4 CUPS QUINOA FLOUR	1/3 CUP ORGANIC RAW BLUE AGAVE, REGULAR, BERRY OR CHOCOLATE
¼ CUP ARROWROOT FLOUR	
½ CUP RAW ORGANIC COCOA POWDER	½ CUP UNSWEET ORGANIC APPLESAUCE (STORE-BOUGHT OR HOMEMADE FROM JUICE PULP)
2 ¼ TBSP TAPIOCA FLOUR	
1 ¼ TSP BAKING SODA	
2 TSP CREAM OF TARTAR	1 TBSP GF VANILLA OR ALMOND EXTRACT
1 ¼ TSP XANTHAN GUM	½ CUP COCONUT OIL
1 TSP SALT	½ CUP VERY HOT WATER
	½ CUP ALMOND BUTTER (OPTIONAL)

Directions

1. Preheat Oven 325 degrees.
2. Grease a 13X9 pan thoroughly or prepare papers for muffin tin.
3. In a medium bowl, combine all dry ingredients together.
4. Add wet ingredients one by one until smoothly blended.
5. Spoon into muffin pan or spread evenly into baking pan.
6. Spoon almond butter in globs over top of brownies.
7. Bake 15-20 minutes, check for doneness with toothpick. If necessary bake another 5-10 minutes.

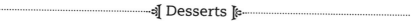

Chillaxin' Brownies

SUGAR FREE, VEGAN

These brownies are the best for "chillaxin" at home. You will start by following the basic brownie recipe on page 50. But before you do that, you need to start preparing the special chillax coconut oil. I wouldn't recommend operating a motor vehicle after either incase you are too relaxed. ☺

Serves 12-16 » Prep Time 5 minutes » Cook Time 20 minutes

½ CUP COCONUT OIL

2 TBSP KAVA KAVA

2 TBSP ST. JOHNS WORT

BASIC BROWNIE RECIPE ON PAGE 50

Directions

1. Preheat Oven 325 degrees.
2. Put Coconut oil in pot and start melting over low-medium heat on stove.
3. Add the Kava Kava and St Johns Wort in the melted oil and stir periodically on low heat for 15-20 minutes.
4. Set aside and allow to cool.
5. Add in coconut oil when it is called for in the basic brownie recipe
6. Bake accordingly.

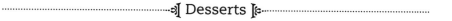

Pure Energy Brownies

SUGAR FREE, VEGAN

Rather than have the brownies that chill you out, heres a new twist to give you a little energy instead. These are great for when you need a pick-me-up, or if you are pushing your limits on the trail, the yoga mat, or just need a plain ole energy boost. It gives your body and brain a little clarity, focus and stamina. If you haven't heard of the herb Moringa, I highly suggest you research and try it. It is considered the tree of life and will give energy and stamina to the body. I do sell it on my website at www.holisticnaturalsco.com. Use the basic brownie recipe on page 50 and add in the oil when it's called for.

Serves 12-16 » Prep Time 5 minutes » Cook Time 20 minutes

½ CUP COCONUT OIL

2 TBSP MORINGA OR SIBERIAN GINSENG

2 TBSP GINGKO BILOBA

BASIC BROWNIE RECIPE ON PAGE 50.

Directions

1. Preheat Oven 325 degrees
2. Put Coconut oil in pot and start melting over low-medium heat on stove.
3. Add the Moringa or Siberian Ginseng and Gingko Biloba in the melted oil and stir periodically on low heat for 15-20 minutes.
4. Set aside and allow to cool.
5. Add in herbal coconut oil, in exchange for Coconut oil when it is called for in the basic brownie recipe.
6. Bake accordingly to basic brownie recipe on page 50.

Chocolate Mousse

SUGAR FREE, VEGAN, RAW FOOD

This chocolate mousse is to die for. It is extremely rich and high in antioxidants. The mystery ingredient, avocado always has people guessing and pleasantly surprised that it isn't made from dairy. This is my favorite raw food treat. You can of course substitute the raw cocoa powder for regular, but please don't ruin it by using what I call chemical maple syrup made with HFCS (High Fructose Corn Syrup), because then it is no longer raw. Kids love this treat! If the cocoa is too strong for the little ones, simply use a little less. Spoon into baby food jars to store. These make perfect serving sizes and are easy for school lunches and on the go.

Servings 6-8 » Prep Time 5 minutes » Cook Time NONE

Dry Ingredients	Wet Ingredients
½ CUP ORGANIC RAW COCOA POWDER.	1 CUP ORGANIC GRADE A OR B REAL MAPLE SYRUP 2 AVOCADOS

Directions

1. Cut Avocados in half, remove the seeds.
2. In a blender or food processor put all 3 ingredients.
3. Blend until smooth.
4. Spoon into individual cups and enjoy!

Key Lime Tarts

RAW FOOD, VEGAN, NO SUGAR

I grew up in Florida, so one of my all time favorite pies is Key Lime Pie. Since I don't do gluten or dairy anymore; I had to learn to recreate my favorite dessert and decided to do it the Raw way. Key Limes have the specific taste of the tropics that makes them special, but if you don't have them in your area, regular limes will do. The macadamia nut crust adds a nice richness, but if you prefer, you can simply serve this in a cup, like a lime pudding.

Servings 8 » Prep Time 40 minutes » Cook Time None

Macadamia Crust Ingredients

2 CUPS OF RAW MACADAMIA NUTS CHILLED

1 CUP RAW UNSWEET SHREDDED COCONUT

¾ TBSP LIME ZEST

2 ½ TBSP LIME JUICE

1 VANILLA BEAN SCRAPED OR 3 TSP VANILLA EXTRACT

1 TSP SEA SALT

4 TBSP RAW BLUE AGAVE

3 TBSP COCONUT BUTTER

1 TBSP MACADAMIA, COCONUT OR OLIVE OIL

Lime Filling Ingredients

3 AVOCADOS, PITTED

2 1/2 TBSP COCONUT BUTTER

2 TBSP LIME ZEST GRATED

1/3 CUP LIME JUICE

2/3 CUP RAW AGAVE

1 VANILLA BEAN SCRAPED OR 3 TSP VANILLA EXTRACT

¼ TSP SEA SALT

Directions for Macadamia Crust:

1. Put all ingredients except for the last TBSP of oil in food processor and mix well, but leave a little chunky.
2. Divide TBSP of Oil between 4 crust tart pans and grease well.
3. Cover with plastic or parchment paper and freeze to make firm until filled.

Directions for Lime Filling:

1. Cut Avocados in half, remove seeds.
2. Put all ingredients in a blender or food processor and blend until smooth.
3. Spoon into individual cups or tart crusts. Chill more if desired.

Macaroon Mounds

SUGAR FREE, VEGAN, RAW FOOD

Oh how I love macaroons! I used to eat them until I got sick to my stomach from all the eggs and sugar. I decided no more tummy aches, I had to master a raw food version, and boy did I succeed. We now have Chocolate, Blondie and my new favorite the Ying Yang a mixture of both. If you want to make Ying Yang, half each of the recipes unless you want a LOT of treats…Trust me they will go fast and they store well if not.

Approx 48 pieces » Prep Time 30 minutes » Dehydrate Time 15-24 hrs

Dry Ingredients for Chocolate

3 CUPS DRIED UNSWEET COCONUT FLAKES

1 ½ CUPS RAW CACAO POWDER OR CAROB

¾ TSP SEA SALT

Wet Ingredients for Chocolate

¾ CUP PURE ORGANIC MAPLE SYRUP

¼ CUP ORGANIC RAW BLUE AGAVE

1/3 CUP COCONUT OIL

1 ½ TBSP VANILLA EXTRACT OR 1 RAW VANILLA BEAN SCRAPED

Dry Ingredients for Blondie

3 CUPS DRIED UNSWEET COCONUT FLAKES

1 ½ CUPS RAW ALMOND OR PECAN FLOUR

¾ TSP SEA SALT

1 CUP DRIED CHERRIES

Wet Ingredients for Blondie

¾ CUP PURE ORGANIC MAPLE SYRUP

¼ CUP ORGANIC RAW BLUE AGAVE

1/3 CUP COCONUT OIL

1 ½ TBSP ALMOND EXTRACT OR 1 RAW VANILLA BEAN SCRAPED

Directions for Chocolate or Blondie:

1. Choose Chocolate or Blondie… Mix all ingredients together.
2. Drop small teaspoonfuls on dehydrator sheets and shape into circles.
3. Dehydrate 15-25 hours on 115 degrees to keep raw.

Directions for Ying Yang Treats:

1. Make both Chocolate and Blondie recipes.
2. Drop small half teaspoonfuls on dehydrator sheets and shape into circles, making an S shape. Put 1 cherry on each side of light and dark.
3. Dehydrate 15-25 hours on 115 degrees to keep raw.

Frozen Fruit Sorbets

NO SUGAR, VEGAN, RAW FOOD

These recipes are a delicious light treat on their own. A scoop of almond butter and Chocolate Agave syrup can be added for more filling but still guilt-free treats! Mix and match your favorites. You can use any of the fruit pulp when you make fresh fruit juice, so you don't waste any parts of fruit.

Serves 8-10 » Prep Time 15 minutes » Cook Time None

Berry Ingredients

4 CUPS OF FRESH BERRIES OR PULP STRAWBERRIES, RASPBERRIES, BLUEBERRIES, BLACKBERRIES

¼ CUP RAW AGAVE SYRUP OR HONEY

½ CUP ALMOND MILK OR COCONUT MILK

Lemon Lime Ingredients

1 CUP LEMON OR LIME JUICE AND PULP

2 CUPS APPLES

¼ CUP RAW AGAVE SYRUP OR HONEY

½ CUP ALMOND MILK OR COCONUT MILK

Chocolate Cherry Ingredients

1 CUP CHERRIES OR PULP

2 TBSP LEMON OR LIME JUICE

2 CUPS APPLES

¼ CUP RAW AGAVE SYRUP OR HONEY

½ CUP ALMOND MILK OR COCONUT MILK

¼ CUP RAW CACAO POWDER

Directions

1. Put all ingredients in a blender and puree until well blended.
2. Put in Freezer until solid.
3. To serve, thaw approximately 10 minutes until soft enough to spoon into dishes.

Frozen Mousse Pops

NO SUGAR, VEGAN, RAW FOOD

This is a wonderful recipe for keeping us cool in the summer. Freezing the chocolate mousse allows the avocado to stay fresh longer.

Serves 4 » Prep Time 5 minutes » Freeze Time – 3 hours

Ingredients

1 RECIPE OF CHOCOLATE MOUSSE ON PAGE 55.

Directions

1. Spoon Chocolate Mousse into Popsicle or fun ice cube molds.
2. Freeze until solid. Enjoy

Raw Fruit Pies

NO SUGAR, VEGAN, RAW FOOD

These pies are super easy and quick to make. The most time consuming part is cutting up the fruit, depending on what kind you choose. Cherries usually take the most time because they have to be pitted. This is a very light tasting dessert but you don't need much because the nuts make it so filling.

Servings 6-8 » Prep Time 10 minutes » Cook Time None

Crust Ingredients	*Pie Ingredients*
2 CUPS RAW ALMONDS	**1 ¾ CUPS FRUIT OF YOUR CHOICE PEACHES, CHERRIES, MANGOS, APPLES, STRAWBERRIES, BLUEBERRIES, OR FIGS OR YOUR FAVORITE MIXTURE**
1/3 CUP RAW AGAVE	
¼ TSP SEA SALT	**3-4 TBSP RAW AGAVE**

Directions

1. Put Almonds in food processor or blender and grind finely.
2. Add Agave to almonds, mix well.
3. Press crust mix evenly into a pie pan. Covering bottom and sides evenly.
4. Cut up all fruit in small bite size chunks and cover with agave.
5. Spread fruit over pie crust evenly.
6. Serve immediately or chill for 15 minutes.

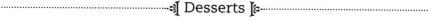

Strawberry Donuts

SUGAR FREE, VEGAN

These strawberry donuts were made with my daughter in mind for Valentines Day so she could have a sweet treat to enjoy. They are topped with a little drizzle of Chocolate Agave and Raspberry Coconut which you don't have to do, but I think it adds a very special flavor to make it complete. I buy the special organic Strawberry extract online from a wonderful company called Herbal Revolution. It is the purest and best I have found. You can of course make these into muffins, too; just don't fill the cups as full.

Serves 12-16 » Prep Time 10 minutes » Bake Time 35-40 minutes

Dry Ingredients

- ½ CUP QUINOA FLOUR
- ½ CUP ARROWROOT FLOUR
- ½ CUP TAPIOCA FLOUR
- 1/3 CUP COCONUT FLOUR
- ¾ TSP CREAM OF TARTER
- 2 TSP XANTHAN GUM
- 1TSP BAKING SODA
- ½ TSP SEA SALT

Wet Ingredients

- ¾ CUP ORGANIC RAW BLUE AGAVE
- 1/3 CUP PLUS 1 TBSP UNSWEET ORGANIC APPLESAUCE (STORE-BOUGHT OR HOMEMADE FROM JUICE PULP)
- 2 TBSP GF VANILLA
- 2 TBSP ORGANIC STRAWBERRY EXTRACT
- 1/3 CUP COCONUT OIL
- ¾ CUP VERY HOT WATER
- ¾ CUP FRESH OR FROZEN STRAWBERRIES, CHOPPED

Topping Ingredients

- 2 TBSP RASPBERRY POWDER
- ¼ CUP UNSWEET COCONUT
- 1 TBSP COCOA POWDER
- ¼ CUP AGAVE SYRUP

Directions for Donuts:

1. Preheat Oven 325 degrees
2. Grease donut pan thoroughly or prepare papers for muffin tin
3. In a medium bowl, combine all dry ingredients together
4. Add wet ingredients one by one until smoothly blended
5. Spoon into donut or muffin pan or spread evenly into baking pan
6. Bake 25 minutes, rotate pan 90 degrees then bake another 10 min, check for doneness with toothpick
7. If necessary bake another 5-10 minutes. Cool completely before topping

Directions for Toppings:

1. Mix Raspberry powder and coconut together, set aside
2. Mix Cocoa and Agave Syrup Together well until all brown.
3. Drizzle Chocolate Syrup over cooled donuts and sprinkle raspberry coconut on top. Freeze leftovers, if any.

Red Velvet Cake

SUGAR FREE, VEGAN

Red Velvet is one of those traditional cakes that are sometimes difficult to match Vegan style due to not using sour milk or chemical laden food dyes. I am most pleased to say that I have done a pretty good job at re-creating this tasty cake, keeping it all natural. Use the icing recipe on page 124. Top with fresh pomegranate seeds or raspberries.

12-16 Servings » Prep Time 20 minutes » Bake Time 50 minutes

Dry Ingredients

1 ½ CUPS QUINOA FLOUR

1 CUP UNSWEET CACOA POWDER

1/3 CUP ARROWROOT FLOUR

1 ¼ TSP BAKING SODA

TSP XANTHAN GUM

2 TSP SEA SALT

1 ½ TSP CREAM OF TARTAR

1 TSP NATURAL FOOD DYE (BEET POWDER, RASPBERRY OR BLACKBERRY)

Wet Ingredients

2 TBSP APPLE CIDER VINEGAR

½ CUP UNSWEET ALMOND MILK

1 ¼ CUP ORGANIC BLUE AGAVE REGULAR OR CHOCOLATE

2/3 COCONUT OIL

2 TBSP VANILLA EXTRACT

Cake Top Decoration

POMEGRANATE SEEDS OR RASPBERRIES FOR TOP

Directions

1. Preheat Oven 350 degrees.
2. Grease cake or donut pans thoroughly, if using a non stick pan then dust with cocoa.
3. Make sour milk by mixing the almond milk and the apple cider vinegar together.
4. In a large bowl, combine all dry ingredients.
5. In a medium bowl, combine sour milk mix and remaining wet ingredients.
6. Add wet ingredients to dry, blending well.
7. Spread evenly in cake or donut pans.
8. For cake bake 25 minutes, rotate pan, bake 20-25 minutes more. For donuts, bake 20 minutes, rotate pan, and bake 20 min more.

Vanilla Cake

VEGAN OPTION

This cake isn't sugar free, but it can be vegan and still taste good. I made this cake for one of the teen girl's birthday and we turned it into the cutest Hello Kitty cut- out covered with pretty white and hot pink fondant. It was a hit at the party, even though it was gluten free. For Frosting Options see Pages 122.

Serves 12-14 » Prep Time 15 minutes » Cook Time 50 minutes

Dry Ingredients	*Wet Ingredients*
1 ½ CUPS QUINOA FLOUR PLUS 1 TBSP FOR FLOURING BAKING PAN	1 CUP COCONUT OIL OR VEGETABLE SHORTENING, PLUS EXTRA FOR GREASING PAN
1 ¼ CUP ARROWROOT FLOUR	1 ORGANIC HORMONE FREE EGG OR 1 ½ TSP VEGAN EGG REPLACER PLUS 2 TBSP WATER
¼ CUP TAPIOCA FLOUR	
1 CUP ORGANIC CANE SUGAR	2 TBSP GF VANILLA EXTRACT
1 TSP SEA SALT	
2 1/4 TSP XANTHAN GUM	

Directions

1. Preheat Oven 375 degrees
2. Grease baking pan of choice, then spread flour to coat pan.
3. In a medium bowl, combine all dry ingredients, omitting sugar
4. In a large bowl, cream coconut oil or shortening with hand mixture until smooth, add sugar, beating well.
5. Add egg or Vegan egg replacer, then vanilla, mixing well.
6. Add dry ingredients to wet little by little until well blended and fluffy.
7. Spread evenly into baking pan, Bake 375 degrees for 40 minutes. Check after 40 min with toothpick to see if it comes clean yet. If not, then continue baking up to the 10 minutes more until toothpick is clean.
8. Let cool in pan for 15 min, then turn onto wire rack and cool at least an hour before adding frosting.

Vanilla Cake Donuts

VEGAN, SUGAR FREE

This is the Vanilla desert option that has no sugar. You can dress it up with icing or just have a plain cake donut to enjoy. For different Vegan Icings, see page 124.

Serves 12-14 » Prep Time » 10 minutes » Cook Time 30-45 minutes

Dry Ingredients

½ CUP QUINOA FLOUR

½ CUP ARROWROOT FLOUR

½ CUP TAPIOCA FLOUR

1/3 CUP COCONUT FLOUR

¾ TSP CREAM OF TARTER

1 TSP XANTHAN GUM

1TSP BAKING SODA

½ TSP SEA SALT

Wet Ingredients

¾ CUP ORGANIC RAW BLUE AGAVE

1/3 CUP PLUS 1 TBSP UNSWEET ORGANIC APPLESAUCE (STORE-BOUGHT OR HOMEMADE FROM JUICE PULP)

3 TBSP GF VANILLA

1 TBSP ALMOND EXTRACT

1/3 CUP COCONUT OIL

¾ CUP VERY HOT WATER

Directions

1. Preheat Oven 325 degrees.
2. Grease donut pan thoroughly or prepare papers for muffin tin.
3. In a medium bowl, combine all dry ingredients together.
4. Add wet ingredients one by one until smoothly blended.
5. Spoon into donut or muffin pan or spread evenly into baking pan.
6. Bake 20 minutes, rotate pan 90 degrees then bake another 15 min, check for doneness with toothpick.
7. If necessary bake another 5-10 minutes. Cool completely before topping.

Dinners

BLACK BEAN BOWL

FIVE BEAN CHILI

MEXICAN PIZZA

GARDEN PIZZA

GREEK PIZZA

ASIAN STYLE FRIED QUINOA

EGGPLANT PARMESAN

STUFFED ROASTED TOMATOES

RAW PASTA MARINARA

BLACK BEAN QUINOA PATTIES

ROASTED SPAGHETTI SQUASH

VEGGIE LENTIL STEW

STUFFED ACORN SQUASH

VEGGIE POT PIE

SPINACH & PUMPKIN RAVIOLI

Black Bean Bowl

VEGAN

This meal is very filling and has a nice variety of flavors to create a party in your mouth. Add to this the recipes for **Fresh Salsa on page 134, Guacamole on page 131 and or Mango Chutney on page 138,** or all three together. You can put them in a bowl together or in the **Basil Coconut Wrap on page 28**. If you don't care for black beans you can always substitute for any other kind of bean you like; (pinto, adzuki, kidney, garbanzo, cannellini, etc).

Serves 8-10 » Prep Time 10 minutes » Cook Time 20 minutes

Ingredients

1 CUP UNCOOKED QUINOA

2 CUPS OF VEGGIE STOCK

2 CAN OR 3 CUPS OF BLACK BEANS OR BEAN OF YOUR CHOICE

1 ½ TBSP OLIVE OIL

1 MEDIUM ONION, CHOPPED

5-6 CLOVES OF GARLIC, MINCED OR PRESSED

2 TSP CUMIN

1 ½ TSP SEA SALT

2 CUPS LETTUCE OR RAW SPINACH CHOPPED (OPTIONAL)

1 CHIPOTLE PEPPER DESEEDED (OPTIONAL)

¼ CILANTRO CHOPPED FOR TOPPING

(OPTIONAL)

Directions

1. Bring Quinoa and water to a boil, stir well and turn down to medium heat, cover and cook 20 minutes, fluff with fork, cover and set aside.
2. While quinoa is cooking, heat pan with oil and cook onions and garlic on medium until onions are clear. Add beans, salt and cumin, & chipotle stirring frequently for 10 minutes. Cover beans and set aside.
3. In a bowl or a wrap, add layer of quinoa, then layer of beans, layer of of Fresh Salsa, Mango Chutney, Guacamole or all 3.
4. Top with lettuce, spinach, cilantro or all.

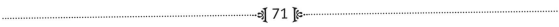

Five Bean Chili

VEGAN

I love my chili, but found I couldn't always eat it because of the high acidic factor. I have found eating some enzymes or drinking a kombucha tea beforehand helps you to enjoy this without the heartburn. I have also omitted ingredients that really contribute to heartburn or cause a lot of mucus. Believe it or not kidneys beans are high on the list of foods that cause mucus and it is considered mildly acidic. You can do it the easy way and go with the BPA-free canned beans. Or even better, if you have the time, soak your own beans. Use 1 ¾ Cup of soaked beans per can.

Makes Approx 8-10 » **Prep Time 20 minutes** » **Cook Time 45 min to 1 hour**

Ingredients

1 CAN ORGANIC FAVA BEANS	OR 4 CUPS OF FRESH CUT & 1 CUP WATER
1 CAN ORGANIC BLACK BEANS	
1 CAN ORGANIC PINTO BEANS	1-2 CHIPOTLE PEPPERS OR 1 TSP DRIED POWDER
1 CAN ORGANIC CANONNELI BEANS	1 JALAPENO PEPPER (DESEEDED)
1 CAN ORGANIC ADZUKI BEANS	1 TBSP CHILI POWDER
	2 TSP SEA SALT
1 6OZ CAN ORGANIC TOMATO PASTE	1 CUP DICED YELLOW ONION
GREEN BELL PEPPER (DESEEDED AND MINCED)	6 FRESH CLOVES OF GARLIC OR 3 TSP MINCED GARLIC
3 14.5 OZ CANS ORGANIC DICED TOMATOES	4 TBSP OLIVE OIL
	3 CUPS OF WATER OR VEGGIE STOCK

Directions

1. In a large stockpot, heat olive oil on medium heat, add onions, garlic, chipotle, jalapeno, green pepper, sauté until translucent.
2. Open all cans or if you are using fresh, add rest of ingredients, bring to a medium boil, stirring frequently.
3. Cover and cook med/low heat for 45 minutes to 1 hour. The longer and slower it cooks the more the flavors enhance.

Mexican Pizza

VEGAN OPTION

This is a great way to spruce up the plain ol' pizza crust Mexican style. Just use **the Pizza Crust** recipe on page 25.
Makes 2 small pizza crusts or 1 large

16 Servings » Prep Time 20 minutes » Cook Time » 15 minutes

Ingredients

PIZZA CRUST RECIPE BAKED ABOUT 10 MINUTES

1 CUP BLACK BEANS

3 ROMA TOMATOES SLICED ½ INCH THICK

3-4 SMALL CLOVES OF GARLIC, MINCED OR PRESSED

¾ CUP CILANTRO CHOPPED

1/4 CUP GREEN ONION, CHIVES OR SCALLIONS, CHOPPED

1 PACKAGE CHEDDAR OR JACK REGULAR CHEESE OR VEGAN DAIYA CHEESE

1 1/2 TSP SEA SALT

1 TSP CUMIN

2 TBSP OLIVE OIL

1 AVOCADO, SLICED

Directions

1. Preheat oven to 400 degrees.
2. Slice tomatoes, onions, chop cilantro, mince or press garlic, slice avocado.
3. Mix olive oil and garlic, spoon or brush evenly on pizza crust.
4. Arrange tomatoes, black beans, onions or chives, and cilantro on top of garlic oil mix. Sprinkle salt and cumin over veggies.
5. Sprinkle Daiya cheese over veggies.
6. Bake 15 min until cheese is melted.
7. Add Avocado slices after comes out of oven.

Garden Pizza

VEGAN OPTION

You will need one **Pizza Crust** recipe from page 25. You are welcome to substitute your own veggies and get creative.

6-8 Servings » Prep Time 15 minutes » Cook Time 15 Minutes

Ingredients

3 ROMA TOMATOES SLICED ½ INCH THICK

¼ GREEN OR RED BELL PEPPER SLICED THIN

1 SMALL YELLOW OR RED ONION SLICED THIN

2 CUPS CHOPPED SPINACH OR ARUGULA OR MIX OF BOTH

8-10 FRESH BASIL LEAVES CHOPPED OR 2 TSP DRIED

1 PACKAGE MOZZARELLA OR DAIYA CHEESE

1 1/2 TSP SEA SALT

2 TBSP OLIVE OIL

4-5 SMALL CLOVES OF GARLIC, MINCED OR PRESSED

Directions

1. Preheat oven to 400 degrees.
2. Slice tomatoes, peppers, and onions, chop basil and spinach, mince or press garlic.
3. Mix olive oil and garlic, spoon or brush evenly on pizza crust.
4. Arrange tomatoes, onions, peppers, basil and spinach on top.
5. Sprinkle Mozzarella or Daiya cheese over veggies.
6. Bake 15 min until cheese is melted.

Greek Pizza

VEGAN OPTION

You will need one already slightly baked **Pizza Crust** recipe from page 25. A yummy treat from the Mediterranean!

6-8 Servings » Prep Time 10 minutes » Cook Time 15 minutes

Ingredients

PIZZA CRUST RECIPE BAKED ABOUT 10 MINUTES

3 ROMA TOMATOES SLICED ½ INCH THICK

1 CAN 13.75 OZ MEDITERRANEAN ORGANIC ARTICHOKE HEARTS

1 12 OZ CAN OR JAR OF MEDITERRANEAN ORGANIC KALAMATA OLIVES

1 LEEK, GREEN AND WHITE PARTS CHOPPED

1/4 CUP RED ONION SLICED THIN

2 CUPS CHOPPED SPINACH

1 SPRIG OF FRESH OREGANO OR 1 TSP DRIED

1 PACKAGE MOZZARELLA OR DAIYA CHEESE

1 1/2 TSP SEA SALT

2 TBSP OLIVE OIL

4-5 SMALL CLOVES OF GARLIC, MINCED OR PRESSED

Directions

1. Preheat oven to 400 degrees.
2. Slice tomatoes, onions, leeks, artichokes, chop oregano, mince or press garlic.
3. Mix olive oil and garlic, spoon or brush evenly on pizza crust.
4. Arrange tomatoes, leeks, artichokes, onions, oregano and spinach on top.
5. Sprinkle Mozzarella or Daiya cheese over veggies.
6. Bake 15 min until cheese is melted.

Asian Style Fried Quinoa

VEGAN OPTION

Oh how I covet Chinese food. Yes, its normally full of gluten and MSG, but it doesn't have to be. This is a wonderful healthy alternative and can be prepared vegan by omitting the egg. Serve it with Asian Stir Fry Vegetables on page 108 and you have a very large meal for many people. This one takes a lot of time if you are you are doing it alone and can go a lot quicker with a little help from a friend or loved one.

Serves 8-10 » Prep Time 30 minutes » Cook Time » 45 minutes

Ingredients

1 CUP UNCOOKED QUINOA	2 TBSP SESAME SEEDS
2 CUPS WATER	2 TBSP CHOPPED GREEN ONIONS OR CHIVES
1/3 CUP YELLOW ONION CHOPPED	
2 CLOVES OF FRESH GARLIC OR 2 TSP OF MINCED	3 LARGE CARROTS PEELED AND FINELY CHOPPED
¼ CUP ORGANIC TAMARI, GLUTEN FREE SOY SAUCE	1 CUP SNOW PEA PODS OR SWEET PEAS
3 TBSP & 1 ½ TSP OLIVE OR COCONUT OIL USED SEPARATELY	2 EGGS & 1 TBSP WATER – OMIT IF VEGAN
	1 TSP SEA SALT IF DESIRED

Directions

1. Put uncooked quinoa and water in a pan and bring to a boil, stir, turn heat down, cover and cook for 15-20 min. Set aside. (While this is cooking chop veggies.)
2. Beat eggs and 1 TBSP water with fork until scrambled well, fry eggs in 1 ½ tsp oil like an omelet a few minutes and flip, cook other side few minutes, remove from burner and cool, chop into small cubes and set aside.
3. In a large fry pan or wok, start to sauté the carrots in the 3 TBSP oil since they take the longest to cook. Add onions, garlic and peas until onions look translucent.
4. Add the quinoa, mix well, add eggs, sesame seeds, salt, soy sauce and continue mixing well.

Eggplant Parmesan

VEGAN OPTION

Eggplant Parmesan is one the Italian family staples. I usually end up making both kinds at the same time to appease the whole family. Then I freeze any leftovers, in single serve containers. It makes a wonderful quick meal when you don't feel like cooking.

Serves 10-12 » Prep Time 15 minutes » Cook Time 45 minutes

Ingredients

- 1 LARGE EGGPLANT, SLICED APPROX ¼ INCH THICK
- 5-6 PIECES OF GLUTEN FREE BREAD
- 1 TBSP OREGANO OR 1 TSP DRIED
- 1 TBSP THYME OR 1 TSP DRIED
- 1 TBSP BASIL OR 1 TSP DRIED
- 4-5 CLOVES OF GARLIC, PRESSED OR MINCED

- 1 MEDIUM YELLOW ONION MINCED
- 1 ½ TSP SEA SALT
- 3 TBSP OLIVE OIL, DIVIDED IN HALF
- 4 CUPS OF TOMATO SAUCE JARRED OR FRESH RAW MARINARA ON PAGES 65 AND 66.
- 2 CUPS FRESH MOZZARELLA OR DAIYA VEGAN CHEESE

Directions

1. Preheat Broiler, grease cookie sheet and toast the bread.
2. Put eggplant on cookie sheet, lightly brush 1 ½ TBSP oil over them evenly on both sides and broil for 3-5 minutes until light brown. Turn oven down to 375.
3. Crush the bread into crumbs into a small bowl; add herbs and salt to mix.
4. In a pot or saucepan, heat remaining 1 ½ TBSP oil on medium and sauté onions and garlic, add tomato sauce, stir continuously for 8-10 min.
5. In a 9"X13" baking dish, spoon some sauce on bottom. Add a layer of eggplant, and sprinkle breadcrumb mixture over top and sprinkle a layer of cheese. Starting again with tomato sauce, repeat the process until no more ingredients are left.
6. Bake 30 minutes until light brown on top. Serve hot.

Stuffed Roasted Tomatoes

I went into the mountains in my camper for a couple of months and decided to crack down on writing this cookbook. One night, I was having a craving for Italian and Mexican both, and couldn't decide what I wanted to make. So I made both and combined them. I am happy to say this turned out great and it just may be one of my new dinner favorites.

6-8 Servings » Prep Time 10 minutes » Cook Time 1 Hour

Ingredients

6 TOMATOES

1 CUP UNCOOKED QUINOA

2 CUPS OF WATER OR VEGGIE STOCK

1 ½ CUP OF FRESH OR 1 CAN BLACK BEANS

4 CLOVES OF GARLIC

2 SHALLOTS MINCED

4 LEAVES OF FRESH BASIL OR 1 TSP DRIED

¼ CUP CILANTRO CHOPPED

2 TBSP PLUS 2 TSP OLIVE OIL DIVIDED

¾ TSP SEA SALT

1 CUP OF MOZZARELLA OR ½ BAG OF DAIYA CHEESE, ABOUT 1 CUP

Directions

1. Preheat Oven 450 degrees.
2. Cut out center of tomatoes, put aside for sauté mix.
3. Rub 2 tsp olive oil all over tomatoes and put in baking dish, bake 15 minutes until soft.
4. Cook Quinoa in water or veggie stock on high until boiling. Turn to medium low setting and cover and cook 20 minutes. Set aside.
5. Sautee minced veggies in 2 TBSP Olive Oil about 5 minutes, add the black beans cook another 5-8 min. Add Cilantro, basil and quinoa and mix well.
6. Spoon quinoa bean mix into tomatoes packing the mixture tight. Pack in any leftover quinoa mix in between the tomatoes.
7. Sprinkle with cheese and bake about 10 minutes until cheese is melted.

Raw Pasta Marinara

VEGAN, RAW FOOD

What an amazing dinner full of flavor and live enzymes! It is quite satisfying to the body and won't make you unbutton your pants like normal pasta does. Fresh herbs really make this recipe pop! If you don't have fresh herbs, dried will work nicely.

3-4 Servings » Prep Time 10 minutes » Cook Time 0-10 minutes

Ingredients

6-7 ROMA TOMATOES OR 4 BEEFSTEAK TOMATOES

3-4 CLOVES OF GARLIC

1/3 CUP CHOPPED YELLOW OR RED ONION

5 BASIL LEAVES (FRESH) OR 1 ½ TSP DRIED

1 SPRIG OF OREGANO OR 1 ½ TSP DRIED

1 ZUCCHINI

Directions

1. Put first 5 ingredients in Blender and Puree.
2. Peel Zucchini and either use a spiral slicer to make curly noodles or use cheese grater and grate vertically in long strokes.
3. If you leave the zucchini out for a few minutes it will become more pliable like a noodle.
4. You can serve this cold or you can put on a low heat setting so it doesn't ruin the enzymes. Heat must not go over 115 degrees.

Black Bean Quinoa Patties

VEGAN

These Quinoa patties make a great veggie burger. Most of the veggie patties on the market contain gluten and mushrooms. I am allergic to both. That prompted me to perfect this recipe. My husband loves his meat, yet actually "digs" these patties. He said they taste really close to a good steak burger. Serve on Gluten free bread or no bread and add a side of vegetables or veggie juice. If you want to bake instead of fry them, preheat oven 350, grease cookie sheet, bake 20 min, flip and bake 10 minutes more until crispy.

4-6 Servings » Prep Time 15 minutes » Cook Time 35 minutes

Ingredients

1 CUP REGULAR OR RED QUINOA	1 TSP SALT
1 CAN ORGANIC BLACK BEANS OR 2 CUPS FRESH SOAKED BLACK BEANS	¼ TSP CELERY SALT
2 CUPS WATER OR VEGGIE BROTH	1 TSP CUMIN
¼ CUP CHOPPED FRESH CILANTRO	1 TSP PAPRIKA
1 MEDIUM YELLOW OR RED ONION CHOPPED	⅛ TSP CRUSHED OR GROUND RED PEPPER
	3 TBSP BELL PEPPER (OPTIONAL)
¼ CUP TOMATOES DICED	1-3 TBSP OLIVE OIL FOR COOKING
4-5 CLOVES GARLIC MINCED	½ CUP WATER

Directions

1. Bring water or veggie broth to a boil in a medium pot.
2. While wait for water to boil Chop Onion, pepper, tomato, Cilantro and mince the Garlic.
3. Add Quinoa to boiling water and reduce to simmer, cover and cook 15 minutes.
4. In frypan, add chopped onion, garlic, cumin, tomato, salt, red pepper paprika, celery salt, sauté 10 min, add ½ of black beans and ½ cup water, cook until water is evaporated.
5. Put mixture and ½ of cooked quinoa in food processor or a blender, puree.
6. Move to mixing bowl and add rest of black beans, quinoa & cilantro, mix well.
7. Heat 1 tbsp oil in skillet on medium heat, drop in spoonfuls of quinoa mix and flatten with spatula to make patties. Cook about 8-10 minutes on each side, flip and cook additional 8-10 min, making sure they are a bit crispy.

Roasted Spaghetti Squash

VEGAN

For those of you who aren't quite ready to go all the way raw and still want vegan spaghetti this recipe is for you. These seeds are just like pumpkin seeds too, full of nutrients and really good toasted. You can serve up this dish up plain with herbs as a side to your favorite main course. Or you can add the marinara sauce below to make it a whole meal, served with Garlic Herb Cheese Bread on Page 32.

3-4 Servings » Prep Time » 15 minutes » Cook Time 15-20 Minutes

Ingredients	*Marinara Ingredients*
1 LARGE SPAGHETTI SQUASH	6-7 ROMA TOMATOES OR 4 BEEFSTEAK TOMATOES
5-6 CLOVES OF GARLIC	3-4 CLOVES OF GARLIC PRESSED OR CRUSHED
1 TBSP OLIVE OIL	1/3 CUP CHOPPED YELLOW OR RED ONION
3 BASIL LEAVES (FRESH) OR ¾ TSP DRIED	5 BASIL LEAVES (FRESH) OR 1 ½ TSP DRIED
1 SMALL SPRIG OF OREGANO OR ¾ TSP DRIED	1 LARGE SPRIG OF OREGANO OR 1 ½ TSP DRIED
1 TSP SEA SALT	1 PACKAGE OF MOZZARELLA DAIYA CHEESE *OPTIONAL

Directions for Squash:

1. Preheat Oven 400 degrees.
2. Wash Squash well and cut in half vertically.
3. Scoop out seeds, rinse, put on cookie sheet, pat dry for roasting as soon as squash is done) drizzle with olive oil then roast 30 min on 350 degrees.
4. Slice garlic thin, make slits in squash with knife, and insert garlic in slits all over squash.
5. Sprinkle with salt &herbs and drizzle with olive oil, Bake 45 min to 1 hour.
6. Take a fork and scrape down making spaghetti noodles.
7. If you are opting for no marinara, then drizzle olive oil over the scraped squash and sprinkle dried herbs and serve.

Directions for Marinara: Optional **(While the squash is baking prepare Marinara)**

1. Put all ingredients in a blender except the Daiya cheese and puree.
2. Cook on medium/low heat for remaining of time the squash is cooking, approx 15-20 min.
3. Pour marinara sauce over spaghetti sauce.
4. Sprinkle on Daiya Cheese if desired.

Veggie Lentil Stew

VEGAN

This is a great thing to have on a cold day. Most of these recipes call for lamb or chicken, but this is a meatless version and tastes amazing and very filling. Freeze any leftovers for a rainy day. Use a food chopper or processor cuts the prep time down to 5 minutes.

8-10 Servings » Prep Time 5-15 minutes » Cook Time 1 hour 15 min

Ingredients

1 CAN ORGANIC BLACK BEANS

1 CAN ORGANIC PINTO BEANS

1 GREEN BELL PEPPER, DESEEDED AND CHOPPED

1 RED PEPPER CHOPPED

1 MEDIUM YELLOW ONION, CHOPPED

2 CARROTS, PEELED AND CHOPPED

1 MEDIUM ZUCCHINI, CHOPPED

3 14.5 OZ CANS ORGANIC DICED TOMATOES OR 4 CUPS OF FRESH CUT & 1 CUP WATER

2 CUPS OF LENTILS, RED, YELLOW, BROWN OR GREEN, RINSED WELL

1 TSP CUMIN

1 TBSP FRESH BASIL

½ TBSP OREGANO

2 TSP SEA SALT

5 FRESH CLOVES OF GARLIC OR 2 ½ TSP MINCED GARLIC

1 CUP SPINACH CHOPPED

3 TBSP OLIVE OIL

4 CUPS OF WATER OR VEGGIE STOCK

Directions

1. In a large stockpot, heat olive oil on medium heat, start with carrots and lentils, cook approx 8-10 min, then add onions, garlic, green & red pepper, zucchini, then spinach, sauté until soft about 5 minutes. Add spices and stir well.
2. Open all cans or if you are using fresh, add rest of ingredients, bring to a medium boil, stirring frequently.
3. Cover and cook med/low heat for 45 minutes to 1 hour. The longer and slower it cooks the more the flavors are enhanced.

Stuffed Acorn Squash

VEGAN

These are delicious little individual pieces of heaven. They are quite filling, so if you must have something to go along with it, then just a simple salad will do.

4 Servings » Prep Time 15 minutes » Cook Time 90 minutes

Ingredients

4 SMALL ACORN SQUASH	1 CUP SPINACH OR BOK CHOY
1 CUP UNCOOKED QUINOA	4 TBSP OLIVE OIL DIVIDED
2 CUPS OF WATER OR VEGGIE STOCK	½ CUP COOKING SHERRY OR WHITE WINE
4-5 CLOVES OF GARLIC	4-5 SAGE LEAVES OR 1 TSP DRIED
¼ CUP YELLOW ONION MINCED	1 SMALL SPRIG OF OREGANO OR ¾ TSP DRIED
¼ CUP CELERY MINCED	1 ½ TSP SEA SALT
¼ CUP CARROTS MINCED	

Directions

1. Preheat Oven 400 degrees
2. Wash Squash well and chop tops off about 1 inch and scoop out seeds, place on foiled cookie sheet. Put ½ TBSP olive oil in bottom of each squash.
3. Rinse and put seeds on cookie sheet, pat dry for roasting as soon as squash is done) drizzle with olive oil then roast 30 min on 350 degrees.
4. Cook Quinoa in water or veggie stock on high until boiling. Turn to medium low setting and cover and cook 20 minutes. Set aside.
5. If you have a food processor, chop all veggies together until minced.
6. Sautee minced veggies in remaining 2 TBSP Olive Oil about 10 minutes.
7. Add white wine or sherry, sprinkle with salt and herbs, add quinoa to mix and stir well.
8. Fill each squash full packing in the mixture tight and putting squash top on, Bake 45 minutes to 1 hour.
9. Don't forget to bake your seeds to enjoy on top while the squash is cooling a few minutes or have another time.

Veggie Pot Pie

VEGAN

I grew up with chicken pot pie and often used to make it from scratch as a child (I was one of those kids who enjoyed cooking when I was bored). This is a wonderful vegan alternative and we can now save those chicks!!! Please remember to use organic ingredients, especially veggies. I encourage you to add in your favorites. Remember, adding corn can technically make this not gluten free, so use discretion.

I have divided this recipe in 2 pages by Crust and Filling. Follow the Crust Recipe first then set aside while you make the filling. You can make one big pie or 6 individual sizes. This is one of the more time consuming recipes so I always love doing it on a rainy day. Remember, using a food processor cuts down prep time. ☺

6 Servings » Prep Time 30-40 minutes » Cook Time 1 hour 10 min

Dry Crust Ingredients	
1 CUP QUINOA FLOUR	**1 ½ TSP SEA SALT**
1 CUP TAPIOCA FLOUR	**½ TSP CREAM OF TARTER**
1 CUP ARROWROOT FLOUR, AND COUPLE EXTRA TABLESPOONS FOR THICKENING DOUGH	**¼ TSP BAKING SODA**
	Wet Crust Ingredients
2 TSP XANTHAN GUM	**1 CUP EXTRA VIRGIN COCONUT OIL (REFRIGERATED FOR EXTRA FIRM)**
	2/3 CUP ICE COLD WATER

Directions for Crust:

1. Preheat oven to 400 degrees.
2. Grease side and bottom of baking dishes.
3. Combine all dry crust ingredients.
4. Add in coconut oil in small teaspoon sizes. Add water and combine well.
5. Divide dough into 6 separate balls, cover and refrigerate for 30 min.
6. If making one big pie, then combine 3 balls for top, and 3 balls for the bottom and knead each of the 3 balls together, set bottom crust into greased baking dish, bake 15 min, set top to the side.
   OR If making 6 separate ones, then divide each of the 6 balls in half for top and bottom, and knead separately, set bottom crust into greased baking dish, bake 15 min, set top to the side.

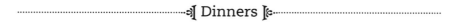

Veggie Filling Ingredients

4 LARGE CARROTS	1 TBSP FRESH OREGANO OR 2 ½ TSP DRIED
1 CUP GREENS (SPINACH, KALE, BOK CHOY, COLLARDS, SWISS CHARD, PEAS OR GREEN BEANS) USE EITHER ONE OR TWO GREENS OR MIX SEVERAL OF THEM TOGETHER	1 TBSP FRESH BASIL OR 2 ½ TSP DRIED
	A DASH OF RED PEPPER FLAKES
	1 ½ TSP SEA SALT
1 MEDIUM YELLOW ONION	½ TSP CELERY SALT
5 CLOVES GARLIC	1 TSP CUMIN
2 SMALL SHALLOTS	1 QUART VEGGIE STOCK
4 STALKS OF CELERY	1 ½ - 2 CUPS WHITE WINE OR COOKING SHERRY
1 LARGE SWEET POTATO, RED OR WHITE POTATO	¼ CUP OLIVE OIL
1 TBSP FRESH SAGE OR 2 ½ TSP DRIED	3 TBSP TAPIOCA FLOUR FOR THICKENING

Directions for Veggie Filling:

1. Cut all Veggies small either by hand or food processor.
2. Sautee carrots and potato or sweet potato in olive oil on medium heat.
3. Add rest of veggies, herbs and spices and sauté.
4. Add white wine and veggie stock, mix well, cook 10 min.
5. To thicken lower heat and add Tapioca Flour, mix well.
6. Spoon Veggie filling into baked crust bottoms.
7. Put on crust top and pinch around with fingers and poke holes with fork.
8. Bake 30-45 minutes until golden brown.

Spinach Ravioli

This is a very simple ravioli recipe. Once you have the Pasta Dough made from page 26, then you fill and press them. You can get a ravioli hand press or pastry cutter to make them. You can choose to put in regular dairy, vegan, or no cheese at all. You can make your sauce really quickly by using the Raw Pasta Marinara recipe on page 83. Like the Old Italian secret goes, if you want a better sauce, allow it to cook slower longer or sit around a day or so for all the flavors to unify together. Not everyone has that kind of time, so do what fits for your timing best.

Serves 4 » Prep Time » 35 minutes » Cook Time 30 minutes

Ingredients

2 POUNDS ORGANIC SPINACH

3-4 CLOVES GARLIC MINCED OR PRESSED

1 SHALLOT MINCED

3 TBSP OLIVE OIL

1 TSP SEA SALT

¼ TSP CRUSHED RED PEPPER

1 RECIPE OF PASTA DOUGH

1 RECIPE OF RAW PASTA MARINARA

1 CUP RICOTTA, MOZZARELLA OR VEGAN DAIYA MOZZARELLA (OPTIONAL)

Directions

1. In a deep fry pan or wok, heat olive oil over medium heat.
2. Add garlic and shallot and red pepper, cook for 3-5 minutes.
3. Add spinach and sea salt, stir and continue stirring until all spinach is wilted.
4. While your spinach is cooking in a medium saucepan, cook on medium low heat your Raw Pasta Marinara. Cook from 15 minutes to 2 hours or desired doneness.
5. Cut your pasta in either 2 inch squares or get a hand press.
6. Fill Ravioli with 2 tsp of cooked spinach and add a pinch or tsp of cheese if desired. Make sure you keep it in the center so it is doesn't leak out.
7. Bring a medium pot of water to a boil.
8. Put the Ravioli top on and press the sides together firmly.
9. Add Ravioli turn down heat to medium and cook for 10-15 minutes.
10. Serve with warm or hot Pasta Marinara.

Pumpkin Ravioli

VEGAN OPTION

This is such scrumptious ravioli! You can use fresh or canned pumpkin. You can serve with the same quick Marinara Sauce on page 83 used in the Spinach Ravioli or serve with crushed garlic, olive oil and basil. Back when I used to eat dairy, my favorite cheese to add to this was Asiago. The closest comparison I have found vegan style is Daiya Havarti. You will need one completed recipe of the Pasta Dough on page 26. Either use a ravioli press or pastry cutter to make cut them out.

Serves 4 » Prep Time » 35 minutes » Cook Time 30 minutes

Ingredients

2 CUPS OF PUMPKIN PUREE

4-5 CLOVES GARLIC MINCED OR PRESSED

2/3 CUP OF YELLOW ONION MINCED

3 TBSP OLIVE OIL

½ CUP OF VEGGIE STOCK

1 TSP SEA SALT

1 HANDFUL FRESH SAGE OR 2 TSP DRIED

¼ TSP CRUSHED RED PEPPER

1 RECIPE OF PASTA DOUGH

1 RECIPE OF RAW PASTA MARINARA OR

4 TSPB OLIVE OIL, 2 CLOVES MINCED GARLIC AND 2 TSP FRESH BASIL OR 1 TSP DRIED

1 CUP ASIAGO, OR VEGAN DAIYA HAVARTI (OPTIONAL)

Directions

1. In a deep fry pan or wok, heat olive oil over medium heat.
2. Add garlic, onion, and red pepper, cook for 3-5 minutes.
3. Add pumpkin puree, sea salt, and veggie stock stir and continue. Cook another 5 minutes.
4. While your pumpkin puree is cooking in a medium saucepan, cook on medium low heat your Raw Pasta Marinara. Cook from 15 minutes to 2 hours or desired doneness.
5. Cut your pasta in either 2 inch squares or get a hand press.
6. Fill Ravioli with 2 tsp of pumpkin puree and add a pinch or tsp of cheese if desired. Make sure you keep it in the center so it is doesn't leak out.
7. Bring a medium pot of water to a boil.
8. Put the Ravioli top on and press the sides together firmly.
9. Add Ravioli turn down heat to medium and cook for 10-15 minutes.
10. Serve with warm or hot Pasta Marinara or Olive Oil, garlic and Basil.

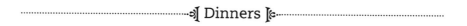

Juices and Smoothies

BERRY GREEN GIANT SMOOTHIE

DARK BERRY FRUIT JUICE

GREEN GO GO JUICE

KAVA CHILL SMOOTHIE

MACACHOCA SMOOTHIE

ORANGE SHERBET

Berry Green Giant Smoothie

SUGAR FREE, VEGAN, RAW FOOD

This smoothie is not green in color but hides your nutritious greens by masking the flavor with berries! It's especially great for those kids and adults that need their greens but don't necessarily like to taste them. The bee pollen is another Super Food and is full of nutrients. Again you can use either avocado or banana. Some people find the banana creates mucus. If this sounds like you then try the avocado instead; you will pleasantly surprised that you won't taste it. Freeze any leftovers so nothing goes to waste and all nutrients are kept for the next time.

Serves 1-2 » Prep Time 5 minutes » Cook Time None

1 BANANA OR AVOCADO

1 ½ CUPS STRAWBERRIES, BLUEBERRIES, RASPBERRIES OR MIX FRESH OR FROZEN

1 CUP OF ALMOND MILK OR RAW COCONUT MILK

1 TBSP RAW BLUE AGAVE

1/3 CUP SPROUTS (ALFALFA, MUNG, BROCCOLI, CLOVER OR MIXTURE)

1 TBSP HEMP, FLAX, CHIA SEED OR MIXTURE (FRESHLY GROUND)

2 TSP BEE POLLEN

1 CUP OF ICE (ONLY IF USING FRESH BERRIES)**

Directions

1. Put all ingredients in blender and blend until smooth.

Dark Berry Fruit Juices

SUGAR FREE, VEGAN, RAW FOOD

These Juice recipes are so good for you, full of antioxidants and are a wonderful way to start the day. Drinking it in the morning is like having a shot of espresso. They make a wonderful frozen sorbet base or you can freeze them into cubes for drinks later. My hubby even likes to use them as the ice in his cocktails. You can make these into a smoothie if you wish by adding ice in the blender.

Serves 1-2 » Prep Time 15 minutes » Cook Time None

Berry Juice Blend	*Tropical Juice Blend*
3 CUPS OF STRAWBERRIES, BLUEBERRIES, RASPBERRIES BLACKBERRIES, CHERRIES (DESEEDED), LOGANBERRIES OR A MIXTURE OF ALL.	**1 PINEAPPLE WITH RIND CUT OFF AND CUT INTO SPEARS.**
4 APPLES SLICED IN CHUNKS	**½ CUP MANGO**
5 CARROTS	**½ CUP STRAWBERRIES**
	2 KIWIS
	1 APPLE
	2 CARROTS

Directions

1. Starting with berries, juice them first, add some apples after, add carrots last.

Green Go Go Juice

VEGAN, RAW FOOD

I call this juice Green Go Go Juice because it gives you a wonderful pick me up to make you GOOOOO! You can feel it going into your veins, making you feel alive again. I drink this one daily. On the rare occasion that I skip this juice, my body will actually feel deprived. I tend to juice once every 3 days. I make enough for it to last the duration. If you share with others it tends to go quicker of course so double or triple up on the recipe. It really helps me to get up and go!

1-2 Servings » Prep Time » 15 Minutes » Cook Time None

Ingredients

5 KALE LEAVES

3-4 SWISS CHARD LEAVES (GREEN, RED OR RAINBOW)

4-5 HANDFULS OF SPINACH

5 APPLES SLICED

2 INCH CHUNK OF GINGER

½ CUCUMBER QUARTERED

3-4 STALKS OF CELERY

12-14 CARROTS

Directions

1. Wash all apples and cucumbers with Veggie Wash due to excess waxes. Others are ok to just wash with water.
2. Cut up apples either using apple slicer or knife.
3. Quarter the cucumber.
4. Juice greens first, adding a few apple slices after each handful of leaves.
5. Juice rest of ingredients in order.

Kava Chill Smoothie

SUGAR FREE, VEGAN, RAW

This is one of those smoothies to have for chillaxin' after a long hard day when you don't feel like cooking. Kava Kava grows in many places, but is most well known in Hawaii. It gives you that special Aloha attitude. It has protein so you don't have to feel guilty about having a shake for dinner.

1-2 Servings » Prep Time » 10 Minutes » Cook Time None

Ingredients

1 BANANA OR AVOCADO

½ CUP PINEAPPLE CHUNKS

½ STRAWBERRIES OR BLUEBERRIES FRESH OR FROZEN

1 CUP OF RAW COCONUT MILK

1 TBSP KAVA KAVA POWDER

1 TBSP HEMP, FLAX, CHIA SEED OR MIXTURE (FRESHLY GROUND)

1 CUP OF ICE IF USING FRESH BERRIES

Directions

1. Put all ingredients in blender and process until smooth.

MacaChoca Smoothie

SUGAR FREE, VEGAN, RAW FOOD

Maca Root is an Inca Superfood that overtones of butterscotch. It is well known for increased stamina, increased libido, & raises energy levels just to name a few. The Maca combined with the cacao (natural chocolate) gives you a vibrant boost for several hours. You have your choice of avocado or banana base. I know it seems like a huge difference in taste but they work as the same binder. Avocado absorbs what you put with it. There is also a significant amount of protein to help keep you balanced and it tastes out of this world! If you have no one to share it with, rather than it going to waste, freeze it so all the nutrients remain until you are ready to have it again.

Serves 1-2 » Prep Time 10 Minutes » Cook Time None

Ingredients

1 BANANA OR AVOCADO

1 CUP STRAWBERRIES OR RASPBERRIES FRESH OR FROZEN

1 CUP OF ALMOND MILK OR RAW COCONUT MILK

½ TBSP RAW CACAO NIBS, BUTTER OR POWDER

½ TBSP MACA ROOT POWDER

1 TBSP HEMP, FLAX, CHIA SEED OR MIXTURE (FRESHLY GROUND)

1 CUP OF ICE IF USING FRESH BERRIES

Directions

1. Put all ingredients in blender and blend until smooth

Orange Sherbet

VEGAN, RAW FOOD

This juice, especially when frozen, tastes just like the orange sherbet that was popular in the 70's and 80's. The funny thing is there is no orange in it at all, but the carrots make it seem that way. It is full of vitamins and minerals, and gives your body a nice little pick me up.

1-2 Servings » Prep Time 10 Minutes » Cook Time None

Ingredients

2 LEMONS PEELED WITH WHITE PART LEFT ON

4-5 APPLES SLICED

10 CARROTS

Directions

1. Juice all ingredients in the order listed.

Lite Bites

APPLE NUT QUINOA SALAD

ASIAN STIR FRY

GREEN BEANS & ALMONDS

GRILLED EGGPLANT

SAUTÉED SPINACH

HERB STUFFING

APPLE NUT STUFFING

SWEET POTATO HASH CAKES

Apple Nut Quinoa Salad

VEGAN

This salad is a wonderful side dish for just about any meal. It is highly nutritious and gives a different flavor to the quinoa than usual by adding the fruit.

8 Servings » Prep Time » 10 minutes » Cook Time 20 minutes

Ingredients

1 CUP UNCOOKED QUINOA

2 CUPS OF WATER OR APPLE JUICE

1 CUP APPLES CHOPPED, GRANNY SMITH, GALA, FUJI, OR GOLDEN DELICIOUS

1/3 CUP OF RAISINS, REGULAR OR GOLDEN

½ CUP ALMONDS OR PECANS

¾ CELERY CHOPPED FINE

¼ CUP LEMON JUICE

1/3 CUP PARSLEY

1/3 CUP GREEN ONION

¾ TSP SEA SALT

½ TSP CINNAMON

3 TBSP OLIVE OIL

2 TBSP HONEY, BRAGGS AMINO ACIDS OR WHITE WINE VINEGAR

Directions

1. Cook quinoa with water or apple juice, bring to a boil, stir, cover and turn down to medium heat. Cook 15-20 minutes. Set aside and cool.
2. Mix lemon juice, honey, vinegar or Aminos with oil and sea salt.
3. Add rest of ingredients to liquid mix, blend well.
4. Add quinoa and mix very well, serve room temperature or chilled

Asian Stir Fry

VEGAN

I was so excited when I discovered Gluten Free Soy Sauce. I was able to start to create my Asian dishes again. After doing some research I found that the mung bean, also known as "bean sprouts" in its raw form is a super body detoxifier. So, the less you cook this recipe the better it is for you. You can use canned mung beans but try to sprout them yourself. It only takes a few days and some water and you can use what you don't cook for an extra detox. This recipe goes great with Fried Quinoa on page 78.

Serves 8 » Prep Time 5 Minutes » Cook Time 10 minutes

Ingredients

2 ZUCCHINI

2 YELLOW SQUASH

3 LARGE CARROTS

1 MEDIUM YELLOW ONION

1 CAN OR 1 CUP OF BEAN SPROUTS (MUNG)

2 CLOVES GARLIC

1 CUP SNOW PEA PODS (OPTIONAL)

2 TBSP OLIVE OIL

3-4 TBSP GLUTEN FREE TAMARIND SOY SAUCE

Directions

1. Chop all veggies except for sprouts and snow pods.
   Put all ingredients except soy sauce in large fry pan or wok on medium heat with oil and continue to stir frequently, cook about 5 minutes
2. Add soy sauce, cook another 3-5 minutes, mix well and serve.

Green Beans & Almonds

VEGAN

Every holiday I am asked to bring this to family dinner. It is our family's favorite. The shallots give it a nice elegant flavor, and the toasted almonds really top it off nicely. Yuummm!!

Serves 4 » **Prep Time** » **5 minutes** » **Cook Time 25 minutes**

Ingredients

1 POUND GREEN BEANS

3-4 CLOVES GARLIC MINCED OR PRESSED

TBSP OLIVE OIL

1 TSP SEA SALT

¼ TSP CRUSHED RED PEPPER

2 SHALLOTS MINCED

2 TBSP YELLOW ONION MINCED

2/3 CUP RAW SLIVERED ALMONDS

Directions

1. Fill a large stockpot 2/3 way full and bring to a boil. Put in steam basket, add the green beans. Steam about 10 minutes.
2. In a deep fry pan or wok, heat olive oil over medium heat.
3. Add garlic, onions, and shallots cook for 3-5 minutes until clear.
4. Add green beans, sea salt, and red pepper stir and continue stirring well, cook about 3-5 minutes.
5. In a dry fry pan, on medium heat add almonds and stir constantly until lightly toasted, about 5 minutes. Put in separate bowl.
6. Serve green beans hot and almonds on top.

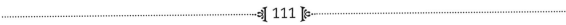

Grilled Eggplant

VEGAN

Living in Florida, you get to use your grill pretty much all year long. This recipe actually came to me in the winter when I was looking for new recipes to create on the grill. It's quick, simple, filling, and can be used as a whole meal or as an appetizer. If you are using a Charcoal grill, remember to start it early before you start prepping.

Serves 4-6 » Prep Time 5 minutes » Cook Time 15 minutes

Ingredients

1 LARGE EGGPLANT OR 4 SMALL JAPANESE EGGPLANTS

3 TBSP OLIVE OIL

2 ½ TBSP BALSAMIC VINEGAR

3-4 CLOVES GARLIC MINCED OR PRESSED

½ TSP SEA SALT

1 ½ TSP DRIED OR 3 TSP FRESH OF BASIL, OREGANO, THYME, AND/OR ROSEMARY.

Directions

1. If using a gas grill, then start it now and put on medium heat.
2. Slice Eggplant approximately ½ inch thick.
3. Mix all other ingredients together pour over eggplant like a marinade, making sure all sides are well soaked.
4. When grill is ready, put eggplant on it and brush remaining juices on top and grill about 5 minutes, flip and brush other side with juices, cook another 10-15 minutes.

Sautéed Spinach

VEGAN

This is a very quick and simple recipe to make. It takes a whole lot of spinach for a small amount, but it sure is worth it. Feel free to add other greens and combine them to the spinach. Kale, arugula, bok choy or swiss chard is great substitute.

Serves 4 » Prep Time » 5 minutes » Cook Time 5 minutes

Ingredients

2 POUNDS ORGANIC SPINACH

3-4 CLOVES GARLIC MINCED OR PRESSED

TBSP OLIVE OIL

1 TSP SEA SALT

¼ TSP CRUSHED RED PEPPER

Directions

1. In a deep fry pan or wok, heat olive oil over medium heat.
2. Add garlic and red pepper, cook for 3-5 minutes.
3. Add spinach and sea salt, stir and continue stirring until all spinach is wilted. Serve hot.

Herb Stuffing

VEGAN

A majority of the gluten free stuffing recipes out there are not vegan friendly. They either call for tons of butter and/or chicken stock. This dish comes with me to all holiday dinners at our family's houses. While everyone else is enjoying their own families' traditional stuffing, my daughter and I can also partake with our yummy treat gluten free vegan style. Remember, using a food chopper or processor cuts the prep time down to nothing.

Serves 8-10 » Prep Time » 5-10 minutes » Cook Time 30 minutes

Ingredients

4 CUPS (PACKED) OF GLUTEN FREE BREAD CUT INTO 1 INCH SQUARES

1 MEDIUM YELLOW ONION CHOPPED

3 STALKS OF CELERY CHOPPED

4 CLOVES OF GARLIC

1 ½ CUPS OF PEELED AND CHOPPED CARROTS

2 ½ TSP FRESH ROSEMARY LEAVES CHOPPED OR 1 ½ TSP DRIED

2 ½ TSP FRESH SAGE LEAVES CHOPPED OR 1 ½ TSP DRIED

2 ½ TSP FRESH THYME LEAVES CHOPPED OR 1 ½ TSP DRIED

2TSP SEA SALT

1 CUP OF VEGGIE STOCK OR WATER WITH VEGGIE STOCK POWER OR CUBES

2 TBSP OLIVE OIL

Directions

1. Chop all bread and veggies into small pieces.
2. Over medium heat, in large pan or wok, put in oil, first sauté carrots for about 5 minutes, then add celery, then add onion and garlic cook another 5 minutes or until soft.
3. Add bread cubes, salt and herbs and stir frequently for a couple minutes, then pour veggie stock over bread and sautéed veggies, add veggie stock and continue to cook and stir frequently for another 10 minutes or until liquid is absorbed.
4. Some desire to then put in oven on 350 degrees for another 10 minutes if you like more dry stuffing.

Apple Nut Stuffing

VEGAN

This is another version of stuffing I attempted for a vegetarian lunch for a class I was holding at my house. I have to admit, I like it better than the traditional herb stuffing and all those at the party loved it too. I like to wow the older ladies who have been cooking for years. It warms my heart to see them swoon over my delicacies!

Serves 8-10 » Prep Time 5-10 minutes » Cook Time 30 minutes

Ingredients

4 CUPS (PACKED) OF GLUTEN FREE BREAD CUT INTO 1 INCH SQUARES

1 MEDIUM YELLOW OR RED ONION CHOPPED

1 CUP OF APPLES CHOPPED

3 CLOVES OF GARLIC

1 CUP OF CHOPPED WALNUTS, PECANS OR ALMONDS

2 ½ TSP FRESH SAGE LEAVES CHOPPED OR 1 ½ TSP DRIED

2 ½ TSP FRESH ROSEMARY LEAVES CHOPPED OR 1 ½ TSP DRIED

1 TSP CINNAMON

2 TSP SEA SALT

1 CUP OF APPLE JUICE

2 TBSP OLIVE OIL

Directions

1. Chop all bread and veggies into small pieces.
2. Over medium heat, in large pan or wok, put in oil, sauté onions, garlic, and apples, cook about 5 minutes or until soft.
3. Add bread cubes, salt and nuts and herbs and stir frequently for a couple minutes, then pour apple juice over bread and sautéed veggies, add veggie stock and continue to cook and stir frequently for another 10 minutes or until liquid is absorbed.
4. Some desire to then put in oven on 350 degrees for another 10 minutes if you like more dry stuffing.

Sweet Potato Hash Cakes

VEGAN OPTION

I do love my starchy potatoes, but they do not love me. Even though they are not considered gluten, the starches aren't great for people with food sensitivities. I used to enjoy the Hash Brown Casserole at Cracker Barrel, but it actually has gluten in it, so that got marked off the list years ago. Sweet Potatoes are an excellent replacement to fulfill the starchy craving and they are quite good for you. If you have a grater attachment on your food processor, this will be grated in a jiff.

Serves 6-8 » Prep Time 5-10 minutes » Cook Time 20 minutes

Ingredients

2 MEDIUM SWEET POTATOES PEELED AND GRATED

1/2 MEDIUM YELLOW ONION CHOPPED

2 TBSP QUINOA FLOUR

2 TBSP ARROWROOT FLOUR

2 CLOVES OF GARLIC, MINCED OR PRESSED

1 TSP SEA SALT

DASH OF CAYENNE OR PAPRIKA

3 TBSP OLIVE OIL FOR COOKING

½ CHEDDAR OR DAIYA CHEESE (OPTIONAL)

¼ CUP CILANTRO OR PARSLEY ON TOP FOR GARNISH (OPTIONAL)

Directions

1. Take the grated sweet potatoes and with either paper towels or an old clean hand towel on top, press down firmly to soak up moisture from potatoes. This decreases the cooking time.
2. Mix all other ingredients in with sweet potatoes except the Oil.
3. Over medium heat, in large pan or wok, heat the oil. Drop spoonfuls of hash into the pan for patties or spread evenly in the bottom of pan. Cook approx 8-10 minutes on medium heat. Flip over and cook another 10 min or until desired doneness.
4. Top with Cilantro or Parsley (optional)

Odds and Ends

EGG REPLACER POWDER

FROSTINGS

ICINGS

NATURAL FOOD DYES

ALMOND BUTTER

SWEETENED CONDENSED MILK

Egg Replacer Powder

Most of the egg replacers on the market are technically not gluten free. Many consist of baking powder which contain cornstarch or potato starch. Neither are great when it comes to food sensitivities. Here is a wonderful alternative that is quick and easy to have on hand for all your baking needs.

Makes approx 3 Cups

Ingredients

2 ½ CUPS OF ARROWROOT FLOUR

¼ CUP CREAM OF TARTER

2 TBSP BAKING SODA

1 TBSP XANTHAN GUM

Directions

1. Combine all ingredients very well and store in airtight container or Ziplock bag until needed. For each egg your recipe calls for replace with 1 ½ tsp of Egg Replacer Powder & 3 TBSP Water. Wisk very well.

Frostings

VEGAN

Oh, how I missed the sweet butter frostings, I could eat it right out of the bowl. Alas! Earth Balance has come up with a wonderful natural buttery spread. Most margarine is only a molecule or two away from being plastic. Although Earth Balance is processed, this spread is vegan friendly and tastes so close to butter in baking. This recipe does have loads of sugar in it, but at least its dairy free!

Makes 2 ½ Cups » Prep Time 5 minutes » Cook Time None

Vanilla Icing Ingredients

½ CUP EARTH BALANCE BUTTERY SPREAD

2 TSP VANILLA EXTRACT OR BEAN

¼ VANILLA ALMOND MILK

3 CUPS ORGANIC CANE SUGAR

¾ CUP TAPIOCA STARCH

Chocolate Frosting Ingredients

½ CUP EARTH BALANCE BUTTERY SPREAD

1 TSP VANILLA EXTRACT OR BEAN

¼ VANILLA ALMOND MILK

3 CUPS ORGANIC CANE SUGAR

¼ CUP TAPIOCA STARCH

½ CUP COCOA, CACAO, OR CAROB POWDER

Strawberry Frosting Ingredients

½ CUP EARTH BALANCE BUTTERY SPREAD

2 TSP STRAWBERRY EXTRACT OR ¼ OF MASHED BERRIES

¼ VANILLA ALMOND MILK

3 CUPS ORGANIC CANE SUGAR

¾ CUP TAPIOCA STARCH

Directions

1. With a hand mixer, blend together the buttery spread and the almond milk, add vanilla or strawberry extract.
2. Put cane sugar and tapioca starch/cocoa in a blender or food processor and grind into a fine powder.
3. Add this powder to the cream mixture, and blend well.
4. Refrigerate about 30 minutes before frosting.

Icings

VEGAN

These icings are yummy and sweet. You can add whatever extracts to them to make them flavored.

Makes 2 ½ Cups » Prep Time 5 minutes » Cook Time None

Vanilla Icing Ingredients

¾ CUP THAI COCONUT MILK
½ ALMOND MILK
¾ CUP COCONUT OIL
1 TBSP LEMON JUICE
2 TSP VANILLA EXTRACT OR BEAN
3 TBSP AGAVE
¼ CUP TAPIOCA STARCH

Chocolate Icing Ingredients

¾ CUP THAI COCONUT MILK
½ ALMOND MILK
¾ CUP COCONUT OIL
1 TBSP LEMON JUICE
1 TBSP CHOCOLATE AGAVE
¼ CUP TAPIOCA STARCH

Strawberry Icing Ingredients

¾ CUP THAI COCONUT MILK
½ ALMOND MILK
¾ CUP COCONUT OIL
1 TBSP LEMON JUICE
2 TSP STRAWBERRY EXTRACT
¼ CUP TAPIOCA STARCH

Directions

1. Mix all ingredients except Tapioca Starch together with hand mixer until blended smoothly.
2. If it is too runny, add 1 Tablespoon more of tapioca starch at a time to thicken.

Natural Food Dyes

These are natural food dyes that are beautiful and fun to make. The best part is there are no chemicals and it you can use them for just about anything, not just food. The juice can be fresh or pureed, but the key is to use dried ingredients, then powder them. The only exception is the greens; the fresh ones are best frozen. Use a dehydrator if you would like to keep the recipe raw making sure you dehydrate at 115 degrees. You will taste a slight flavor, but not at all compared to its original state. It's always a good idea to make all your pretty colors in powder form ahead of time. Then label and store them in airtight jars until ready for use.

Red Ingredients	*Green Ingredients*
BEETS – DEEP RED	**SPIRULINA POWDERED**
RASPBERRIES OR CRANBERRIES – PINK	**MINT, SPINACH OR KALE**
Blue Ingredients	*Yellow, Brown, Orange Ingredients*
BLUEBERRIES – LIGHT BLUE	**TURMERIC – YELLOW**
ELDERBERRIES – DARK BLUE	**COFFEE OR TEA – BROWN**
	CARROT – ORANGE
	TURMERIC & BEET POWDER - ORANGE

Directions

1. Take your fruit or veggie and dehydrate it until completely dry, each item will take different times to dry.
2. Grind the dried product into a powder with coffee grinder.
3. For coloring with flavor, add the dried powder 1 tsp at a time until desired color is achieved.
4. To make the color without using the flavor of the product, use 1 tsp of any powder, add 1 tsp of water, then strain with cheesecloth or clean washrag, and discard powder.

Almond Butter

VEGAN, SUGAR FREE, RAW FOOD

Yes, You can buy raw almond butter, but it is rather pricey. Here is a quick and easy way to keep raw almond butter on hand at home. It is a very healthy snack that can be used with celery sticks, on toast, wraps or crackers, or used in recipes. You can do this with other nuts as well. Most almonds sold are not raw. United States laws prohibit raw almonds. They will still be pasteurized. You can however; find true raw almonds at the health food store from out of the country. They are a bit more money, but worth it if you want to keep things raw.

Makes 2 Cups » **Prep Time 10 minutes** » **Cook Time None**

Ingredients

2 CUPS RAW ALMONDS

1/2 TBSP OLIVE OIL

1 TBSP COCONUT OIL FIRM

1/2 TSP SEA SALT

2 TSP ORGANIC RAW BLUE AGAVE OR HONEY (OPTIONAL)

Directions

1. Grind the nuts in a food processor or juicer with grinding attachment.
2. Add Oils and salt, mix about 10 minutes or so, scraping sides constantly until smooth.
3. If making sweet, add agave or honey. mix well again. Store in glass jars in the refrigerator.

SWEETENED CONDENSED MILK

VEGAN, SUGAR FREE

One thing I missed was a nice vegan alternative to sweetened condensed milk. So I decided to go on the journey to figure out how to make it. I am proud to say I conquered it and a sugar free option too, woohooo! Now you don't have to miss your favorite holiday snacks that called for this devilish ingredient.

Makes 4 Cups » Prep Time 5 minutes » Cook Time 10-15 minutes

Ingredients

2 CANS OF PURE COCONUT MILK OR 3.5 CUPS RAW COCONUT MILK

½ CUP AGAVE

1 TSP GLUTEN FREE VANILLA EXTRACT

Directions

1. Combine all ingredients and cook on low heat until golden brown and thick, stirring continuously. Careful! Agave burns higher than 325 degree. You may want to use a candy thermometer.

Party Favorites

FRESH SALSA

BLACK BEAN SALSA

FRUIT SALSA

GUACAMOLE

NO BEAN HUMMUS

MANGO CHUTNEY

PUMPKIN SEED PATE'

Fresh Salsa

VEGAN, RAW FOOD

This is great snack with sweet potato chips, Black Bean Crackers on page 31 or in Mexican Black Bean Bowl on page 71 or Basil Coconut Wrap on page 28.

Serves 8-10 »   » Prep Time 20 minutes » Cook Time None

Ingredients

2 CUPS TOMATOES CHOPPED

1 LIME SQUEEZED

¼ CUP TOMATOES CHOPPED

3 TBSP YELLOW OR RED ONION CHOPPED

3 CLOVES OF GARLIC PRESSED OR MINCED

¼ CUP CILANTRO CHOPPED

1 TSP SEA SALT

½ TSP CUMIN

Directions

1. Combine all ingredients and mix very well.
2. Chill for 10-15 minutes and serve.

Black Bean Salsa

VEGAN, RAW FOOD OPTION

Black Bean Salsa is a way to spruce up normal salsa and give it a bit of spicy kick. It is served best with Black Bean Crackers on page 31 or in Mexican Black Bean Bowl on page 71 or Basil Coconut Wrap on page 28.

Serves 8-10 » Prep Time 20 minutes » Cook Time None

Ingredients

2 CUPS TOMATOES CHOPPED

½ CUP BLACK BEANS FRESH COOKED OR CANNED

1 LIME SQUEEZED

½ CUP YELLOW ONION CHOPPED OR 4 STALKS GREEN ONIONS

3 CLOVES OF GARLIC PRESSED OR MINCED

¼ CUP CILANTRO CHOPPED

1 TSP SEA SALT

½ TSP CUMIN

1 CHIPOTLE PEPPER DESEEDED AND CHOPPED

Directions

1. Combine all ingredients and mix very well.
2. Chill for 10-15 minutes and serve.

Fruit Salsa

VEGAN, RAW FOOD

This is a delicious light treat when you are craving something to satisfy your sweet tooth. It is served best with a bag of sweet potato chips. Please try to use all organic fruit for this. If you can't do all organic, at least use organic strawberries, as they have the most pesticides.

Serves 8-10 » Prep Time 20 Minutes » Cook Time None

Ingredients

1 LB ORGANIC STRAWBERRIES

¾ CUP BLUEBERRIES

¾ RASPBERRIES.

1 PEACH OR PEAR

1 CUP OF MANGO OR PINEAPPLE

¾ CUP AGAVE

1 TSP FRESH MINT

1 TSP CILANTRO

Directions

1. Mix all ingredients together until well blended. Serve chilled.

Guacamole

VEGAN, RAW FOOD

This is one of the weekly staples in my house. Avocados are so versatile and offer many nutrients especially for vegetarians. I can't it tell you how many times I have given this recipe to friends of mine. I often eat it as a whole meal with sweet potato chips or Black Bean Crackers on page 31. It's wonderful as part of an entire Mexican meal, too, on a Black Bean Bowl on page 71, or just in a wrap with other veggies.

Serves 8-10 » Prep Time 20 minutes » Cook Time None

Ingredients

2 AVOCADOS

1 LIME

¼ CUP TOMATOES CHOPPED

3 TBSP YELLOW OR RED ONION CHOPPED

3 CLOVES OF GARLIC PRESSED OR MINCED

¼ CUP CILANTRO CHOPPED

1 TSP SEA SALT

1 TSP GREEN TABASCO (OPTIONAL)

Directions

1. Mash avocados until somewhat smooth.
2. Add all other ingredients and mix very well.
3. Chill for 10-15 minutes and serve.

No Bean Hummus

When I discovered the beauty of raw foods, I started to recreate those things that my soul loved but my body didn't. Chick Pea/Garbanzo Beans do not settle with my digestion well at all. This alternative uses zucchini which is a great base and replacement for beans. Quick and easy to make, it serves great with Black Bean Crackers on page 31. To keep it raw, serve with raw veggies.

Serves 10-12 » Prep Time 25-30 minutes » Cook Time None

Ingredients

2 ZUCCHINI PEELED & CHOPPED INTO CHUNKS.

¾ CUP RAW TAHINI

½ CUP LEMON OR LIME JUICE, APPROX 2 LEMONS OR 4 LIMES.

¼ CUP OLIVE

4-5 CLOVES GARLIC PRESSED

2 ¼ TSP SEA SALT

½ TBSP CUMIN

1 TSP PAPRIKA

DASH RED PEPPER

Directions

1. Put all ingredients in food processor or blender and puree until smooth.
2. Chill for about 15-20 minutes to allow flavors to blend.

Mango Chutney

VEGAN, RAW FOOD

This yummy treat is big hit at parties. It has a wonderful sweet and sour flavor with a kick of pepper. It works well with Black Bean Crackers on page 31, sweet potato chips, on a salad to dress up the flavor or on a Basil Coconut Wrap on page 28 with some quinoa.

Serves 10-12 » Prep Time » 30 minutes » Cook Time » None

Ingredients

2 CUPS MANGO CHOPPED INTO CHUNKS.

2 KIWI PEELED AND CHOPPED

3 TBSP LEMON OR LIME JUICE

3 TBSP RED ONION MINCED

1 ½ TSP RAW APPLE CIDER VINEGAR

2 TSP OLIVE OIL

3 CLOVES GARLIC PRESSED OR MINCED

½ TSP SEA SALT

2 TBSP DRIED MUSTARD SEED

2 TSP RAW BLUE AGAVE

¾ CUP CHOPPED CILANTRO

¼ CUP YELLOW, RED OR GREEN PEPPER

¼ TSP CAYENNE PEPPER

1/8 TSP MESQUITE

Directions

1. Mix all ingredients together until well blended.
2. Chill for about 15-20 minutes to allow flavors to blend.

Pumpkin Seed Pate'

VEGAN, RAW FOOD

This is a delectable side dish that has the dinner crowds raving. No one ever guesses it is a raw food treat made from raw pumpkin seeds. It can be served with crackers or in a Basil Coconut Wrap on page 28, or as a topping on a bed of greens. If you would like to kick it up a few notches, feel free to add one or both of the following fire options at the bottom.

Serves 10-12 » Prep Time 40 minutes » Cook time None

Ingredients

2 CUPS RAW GREEN PUMPKIN SEEDS

4 CUPS COLD FILTERED WATER FOR SOAKING

¾ CUP PARSLEY

½ CUP CILANTRO

4 CLOVES OF GARLIC

1/3 CUP OLIVE OIL

1 ½ TSP SEA SALT

½ CUP OF LEMON OR LIME JUICE

1 TBSP GINGER GRATED OR MINCED

FIRE OPTIONS

1 Chipotle Pepper deseeded **OR** 1 tsp Jalapeno pepper

Directions

1. Soak the pumpkin seeds in the water for approximately 30 minutes or more.
2. Put all ingredients in a blender or food processor and puree until smooth and creamy. Serve room temperature or chilled.

Soups and Salads

BUTTERNUT SQUASH SOUP

AVOCADO LIME SOUP

FRENCH ONION SOUP

CAPRICCIO SALAD

KALE SESAME SALAD

CREAM OF PUMPKIN ROASTED GARLIC SOUP

PEAR & STRAWBERRY GREEN SALAD

Butternut Squash Soup

VEGAN

This is great for those cold days when you just want to stay inside and be cozy. Serve this with Garlic Herb Cheese Sticks on page 32 and a Salad for a full meal. Another yummy idea is adding a handful of black bean pasta crushing them to make tiny noodle bits. This makes the soup more hearty and full of extra protein. In the rare case you have leftovers; you can freeze it and re-heat a serving or two when you don't feel like cooking.

10-12 Servings » Prep Time » 20 minutes » Cook Time » 1 hour 35 min

Ingredients

1 LARGE BUTTERNUT SQUASH 4-5 LBS.

1 MEDIUM YELLOW ONION

1 LEEK, WHITE PART ONLY

1 WHOLE BULB GARLIC

2 TBSP OLIVE OIL

2 CHIPOTLE PEPPERS (SEEDS OMITTED)

1 TSP MESQUITE

½ CUP HONEY

2 TBSP FRESH CHOPPED SAGE OR 2 TSP DRIED

2 TBSP FRESH ROSEMARY

2 TBSP FRESH THYME OR 2 TSP DRIED

1 TSP SEA SALT

CINNAMON GARNISH FOR THE TOP

Directions

1. Preheat oven 350 degrees.
2. Chop top off garlic bulb, then drizzle on olive oil and wrap in foil, bake 30 min. remove cloves from bulb.
3. Peel, cut up squash in cubes (remove seeds, rinse, pat dry and set aside for roasting as soon as garlic is done) drizzle with olive oil then roast 30 min.
4. Cut up onion, leeks, chipotle peppers, sauté in olive oil in a large stock pot.
5. Add squash, roasted garlic cloves & veggie stock to stockpot.
6. Cook on medium heat about 45 min; reduce to low heat another 20 min.
7. Put all contents in food processor or blender add honey, puree.
8. Sprinkle with cinnamon and serve.

Avocado Lime Soup

VEGAN, RAW FOOD

This is the simplest most delicious soup to make. As a raw food recipe, (meaning it isn't cooked at all) this is one of the healthiest ones in this book. Please make sure you buy organic. Stays good for up to a week, tastes best after flavors sit together a couple hours, but can be eaten right away. Serve chilled.

6-8 Servings » Prep Time » 10 minutes » Cook Time None

Ingredients

2 AVOCADOS

6-7 STALKS OF CELERY (JUICED)

2 SMALL LIMES (JUICED)

2-3 CLOVES GARLIC

¼ CUP OLIVE OIL

1 SHALLOT

1 TSP SEA SALT

¼ CILANTRO FOR GARNISH (OPTIONAL)

Directions

1. Make sure your celery and limes are juiced. Discard pulp.
2. Put juice in blender and puree all ingredients together or mash by hand, sprinkle with cilantro if desired. That's it-isn't Raw Food Awesome??

French Onion Soup

This is one great soup that my husband asks me to make. He isn't a fan of soup at all, but he loves this one. He loves his dairy cheese and bread so I make his traditional of course, but it's nice to have the gluten and dairy free option.

8-10 » Servings » Prep Time 10 minutes » Cook Time » 45 min - 1 hour

Ingredients

3 LARGE YELLOW ONION, SLICED INTO THIN RINGS.

3 CLOVES GARLIC

3 TBSP OLIVE OIL (DIVIDED)

1 HANDFUL FRESH SAGE OR 1 TSP DRIED

1 TSP DRIED THYME

5 CUPS VEGGIE STOCK

1 CUP WATER

2 ½ TSP SEA SALT

¼ WHITE WINE OR COOKING SHERRY

1½ TSP DRIED MUSTARD

8-10 SLICES OF GLUTEN FREE BREAD OR BLACK BEAN CRACKERS

1 CUP OF SLICED OR GRATED GRUYERE, SWISS OR MOZZARELLA CHEESE OR VEGAN DAYIA MOZZARELLA CHEESE

Directions

1. In a large stockpot, take 1 ½ TBSP Olive oil and heat on medium heat, add onions and garlic and sauté until light brown.
2. Add white wine or sherry and cook into onion, then add veggie stock and water.
3. Preheat oven to 350.
4. Add spices to onion mix and cook at low/medium temperature for 45 minutes.
5. Put a piece of bread into the bottom of each bowl for a serving. Place the sliced or grated cheese on top and bake for 10-15 minutes until cheese is melted.

Capriccio Salad

VEGAN

Capriccio Salad is a great treat to make for guests. The Daiya cheese works wonders hot or cold. If you don't have access to Roma Tomatoes, any others will suffice. Dry Basil will work as a replacement, but the fresh is preferred. Some people prefer light Balsamic Vinaigrette and others like it more heavy. The choice is yours.

4-6 Servings » Prep Time » 5 minutes » Cook Time None

Ingredients

3-4 ORGANIC ROMA TOMATOES.

½ CUP MOZZARELLA OR VEGAN DAIYA CHEESE

½ TSP SEA SALT

2-3 TBSP BALSAMIC VINEGAR, RASPBERRY PREFERRED

4-5 FRESH BASIL LEAVES, CHOPPED

Directions

1. Slice the tomatoes about ¼ inch thick and place on serving tray.
2. Sprinkle on Sea Salt, Daiya Cheese and Basil over the tomatoes.
3. Drizzle the Balsamic Vinegar over the tomato mixture.

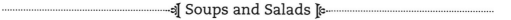

Kale Sesame Salad

SUGAR FREE, VEGAN, RAW FOOD

What a delicious, nutritious, light salad this is! It is quick and simple to make, and is great for the digestion. You can have it served in bowl or my favorite is to add some avocado slices and put it in a Coconut Basil Wraps on page 28. The dressing is what gives it that special flavor.

Serves 6-8 » Prep Time 5 minutes » Cook Time None

Dressing Ingredients

1 Cup Organic Apple Cider Vinegar
¾ CUP EXTRA VIRGIN OLIVE OIL
1 CUP BRAGGS LIQUID AMINO ACIDS
3 TBSP RAW HONEY
2 TSP GINGER, GRATED
2 TBSP SESAME SEEDS
3 TBSP LEMON JUICE
3-4 CLOVE GARLIC PRESSED OR MINCED

Salad Ingredients

1 Cup Cherry or Grape Tomatoes
1 BUNCH OF KALE DEVEINED AND SHREDDED
1 CARROT, PEELED
¼ CUP YELLOW OR RED ONION SLICED IN THIN RINGS.(OPTIONAL)

Directions

1. Mix all dressing ingredients together and chill for 10 minutes.
2. Prepare salad by shredding Kale and add tomatoes sliced or whole, peeled carrots on top and onions if adding.
3. Top with dressing.

Cream of Pumpkin Roasted Garlic Soup

VEGAN

I was born in late October, so my birthday present to myself every year is making Cream of Pumpkin Roasted Garlic Soup topped with toasted Almonds and share it with my friends. Part of the fun is gutting the pumpkin! It moisturizes your hands and strengthens your fingernails while playing in a gooey fun mess. If you are using a fresh pumpkin, don't forget to scoop out those pumpkin seeds and save them to eat later. Don't worry, you don't have to go thru all the mess, you can cheat and buy the Organic Pumpkin Puree if playing with goo isn't fun for you.

10-12 Servings » Prep Time 20 minutes » Cook Time » 1 hour 25 minutes

Ingredients

4 CUPS OF PUMPKIN PUREE

1 MEDIUM YELLOW ONION, MINCED

1 BULB GARLIC

3 TBSP OLIVE OIL (1 FOR ROASTED GARLIC AND 2 FOR SAUTEE)

2 SMALL GREEN ONIONS OR CHIVES

1 HANDFUL FRESH SAGE OR 2 TSP DRIED

1 ½ CUP VEGGIE STOCK

3 CUPS ALMOND MILK

¼ CUP ORGANIC AGAVE SYRUP

1 TSP CRUSHED RED PEPPER

½ TBSP CINNAMON

1 TSP CUMIN

1 CUP SLICED ALMONDS FOR GARNISH (OPTIONAL)

Directions

1. Preheat oven 350 degrees.
2. Chop top off garlic bulb, then drizzle on 1 TBSP olive oil and wrap in foil, bake 30 min. remove cloves from bulb.
3. In a large stockpot, sauté yellow onion, medium heat until onions turn clear.
4. With heat turned down to simmer, add to the stockpot, pumpkin puree, veggie stock, almond milk, roasted garlic and all spices, stir by hand 5 minutes.
5. In a blender, puree all ingredients together until smooth. May have to blend in small batches.
6. Put pureed ingredients back in stockpot, add agave, green onion or chives, simmer on low heat 35-45 min.
7. Put almonds in a dry pan on medium heat, keep stirring them until slightly browned and toasted to your liking. Put them on top of your soup as a garnish and extra protein!

Pear & Strawberry Green Salad

VEGAN, RAW FOOD OPTION

This salad is one of my favorite salads to bring to a spring or summer party. It is nice and light, and easy on the digestion. Because there is fruit in it, kids are usually more apt to eat it as well. Both walnuts and almonds taste great in this salad. In my opinion for this particular recipe, the walnuts taste better raw and the Almonds taste better toasted.

8-10 Servings » Prep Time 10 minutes » Cook Time None

Ingredients

5 OUNCES OF BABY SPINACH

1 ½ CUPS OF ORGANIC STRAWBERRIES SLICED

½ PEAR SLICED THIN

½ CUCUMBER SLICED

1 CARROT PEELED

1 CUP OF WALNUTS OR ALMONDS RAW OR TOASTED

1 BOTTLE RASPBERRY VINAIGRETTE DRESSING

Directions

1. Slice all the fruit and cucumber. Peel the carrot into shavings.
2. Mix spinach, fruit and veggies together
3. Top with Raspberry Vinaigrette and or nuts
4. If you are toasting the nuts; then just put in a pan on medium heat stirring continuously until lightly brown.

Snacks

ABJ ROLL UPS

RAW APPLE SAUCE

RAW BERRY APPLE SAUCE

CINNAMON TOASTED ALMONDS

FRUIT ROLL UPS

FLAX SEED CRACKERS

HAWAIIAN COCONUT BALLS

SWEET CHOCOLATE BALLS

RAW FOOD ENERGY BAR

YE OLE' TRAIL MIX

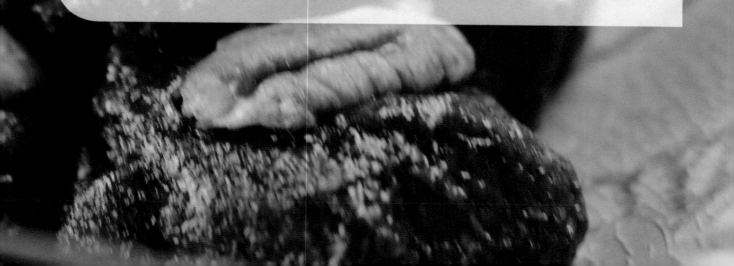

ABJ Rolls Ups

SUGAR FREE, VEGAN, RAW FOOD

Instead of peanut butter and jelly sandwiches that are generally full of sugar and other not-so-good-for-you stuff, I have come up with these amazing treats using almond butter and berries. You can use traditional peanut butter if you wish, but almonds are generally easier on the digestion.

Approx 48-60 pieces » **Prep Time** » **5 minutes** » **Dehydrate Time 8 hours**

Ingredients

1 ½ CUP ALMOND BUTTER

1 PINT OF STRAWBERRIES, BLACKBERRIES OR RASPBERRIES

1 TBSP RAW AGAVE

Directions

1. Puree all ingredients in blender or food processer.
2. Spread thin on dehydrator sheets in small circles and set on 115 degrees. Dry for 8 hours or so until they peel off the sheet.
3. Roll up and enjoy!

Raw Apple Sauce

SUGAR FREE, VEGAN, RAW FOOD

This applesauce is a delicious treat that is so easy to make! I love giving this recipe to babies. They devour it. This can last up to a week in the fridge and forever in the freezer. It make great frozen pops too! If you have one, an apple slicer it makes this task much quicker.

6-8 servings » Prep Time » 10 minutes » Cook Time None

Ingredients

4-5 SMALL ORGANIC APPLES CUT UP

2 CUPS WATER

1 CUP RAISINS, DRIED CRANBERRIES, DATES OR FIGS

¼ OF A SMALL LEMON WITH THE RIND

1 ½ TSP CINNAMON OR A MIX OF ¾ TSP CINNAMON AND ¾ TSP NUTMEG

Directions

1. Puree all ingredients in blender or food processer.

Raw Berry Apple Sauce

SUGAR FREE, VEGAN, RAW FOOD

This is a great alternative to plain applesauce to add a little kick. Feel free to switch any of the berries out with your favorite berry of choice.

6-8 servings » Prep Time 5 minutes » Cook Time None

Ingredients

4-5 SMALL ORGANIC APPLES CUT UP

2 CUPS WATER

1 ½ CUPS OF STRAWBERRIES, BLUEBERRIES, RASPBERRIES, BLACKBERRIES, OR CHERRIES

¼ OF A SMALL LEMON WITH THE RIND

1 ½ TSP DRIED GINGER OR A TINY CHUNK OF FRESH GROUND UP FINE

Directions

1. Puree all ingredients in blender or food processer.
2. Pour into small jars or bowls and serve.

Cinnamon Toasted Almonds

VEGAN

Have you ever been to a festival or sporting event where they sell these divine tasty treats??? Most of them are actually gluten free, but chock full of sugar. These are made from Maple Syrup instead, so it's still sweet but doesn't affect your body, so enjoy guilt free!

Serves » 4 » Prep Time 5 minutes » Cook Time 35 minutes

Ingredients

4 CUPS RAW ALMONDS

2 TSP CINNAMON

½ TSP SEA SALT

1 CUP MAPLE SYRUP

Directions

1. Preheat Oven 375 degrees
2. Mix Maple Syrup, cinnamon and sea salt together and pour over Almonds, coating evenly.
3. Bake in oven about 15 minutes. Pull out, turn almonds over, and bake another 15-20 minutes until golden brown. Serve hot or warm.

Fruit Roll Ups

SUGAR FREE, VEGAN, RAW FOOD

These will bring you back to the days of fruit roll ups before they consisted of having a tongue tattoo. It really sickens me that companies have stooped so low as to have these kids begging their parents to inject cancerous dyes right into their tongues. Glad to report these treats up are straight up hippy style, no red dye 40, blue 1, yellow 5 and yellow 6 here! You can mix and match the fruits of course, but Apples and or Pears are your general base. You will need to get out your dehydrator.

Makes 48-60 pieces » Prep Time » 5 minutes » Dehydrate Time 3-4 hours

Ingredients

4 APPLES

1 PINT ORGANIC STRAWBERRIES

4 KIWIS

1 PINT OF BLUEBERRIES

Directions

1. Put them all into the blender or food processor and puree it together.
2. Drop small circles on the dehydrator trays.
3. Dehydrate on 100 degrees until leathery, approximately 3-4 hours.
4. Peel off sheets, roll up and enjoy.

**Ideas for other fruit variations..
Peaches, pineapple, persimmons, watermelon w/o seeds and rind, raspberries, blackberries, pomegranates.

Flax Seed Crackers

VEGAN, RAW FOOD

These crackers are so yummy and they can become addicting if you are not careful. They are great plain or with **Pumpkin Seed Pate on page 141, Mango Chutney on page 138, Fresh Salsa on page 134, or Guacamole on page 131** just to name a few. You can make them spicy or non spicy. They are great to take on the road to keep your body fed and your mind awake.

10-12 Servings » Prep Time » 10 minutes » Dehydrate Time 9 Hours

Ingredients

2 CUPS OF FLAX SEEDS REGULAR OR GOLDEN (1 CUP WHOLE FLAX, 1 CUP GROUND INTO FLAX MEAL)

1 ½ TBSP OLIVE OIL

1/3 CUP CHOPPED GREEN OR RED BELL PEPPER

1 1/3 CUP TOMATOES, DICED

½ SUN DRIED TOMATOES

¼ CUP YELLOW ONION MINCED

½ CUP FRESH CILANTRO CHOPPED

3-4 CLOVES OF GARLIC, MINCED OR PRESSED

1 1/4 TSP SEA SALT

Directions

1. Puree all ingredients in a food processer EXCEPT for the flaxseeds.
2. Pour puree mixture over flax seeds and mix well.
3. Cut them into shapes if desired. Place on solid dehydrator sheets and dehydrate on 100 degrees for 3-4 hours.
4. Transfer onto a mesh dehydrator tray and dry for another 4-5 hours until the crackers are crispy.

Hawaiian Coconut Balls

SUGAR FREE, VEGAN, RAW FOOD

When my husband and I were in Maui, we found this little farmers market that sold the best organic and raw foods. These little raw food balls were so divine and the perfect pick me up after a long day in the Hawaiian sun, I decided to recreate them to bring back a little Aloha with us. Adding just a little chocolate, vanilla or raspberry, really enhances the flavors, or they are perfect plain!

Serves 10-12 » Prep Time 15 minutes » Cook Time None

Ingredients

2 CUPS OF MEDJOOL DATES PITTED

1 ¾ CUP OF SHREDDED UNSWEET COCONUT FLAKES

3 TBSP AGAVE OR RAW HONEY

2 TBSP RAW CACAO, CAROB OR RASPBERRY POWDER (OPTIONAL)

1 TSP VANILLA BEAN SEEDS OR EXTRACT (OPTIONAL)

Directions

1. Mash dates very well into a paste.
2. In a separate bowl, add 1 Cup of Coconut and rest of ingredients, mix well.
3. Add coconut mix to date paste and blend well.
4. Shape into balls and roll in remaining coconut until fully covered.

Sweet Chocolate Balls

SUGAR FREE, VEGAN, RAW FOOD

These are a great snack to have on hand at home to satisfy your hunger and give you a quick energy boost. They are filled with protein, fiber, and omega 3 fats. Best of all they are a raw food snack!

Makes 24 Balls » Prep Time 30 minutes » Cook Time none

Dry Ingredients	Wet Ingredients
½ CUP RAW CACAO POWDER OR CACAO NIBS POWERED	1 CUP RAW ALMOND BUTTER FROM PAGE 127.
1 TBSP SESAME SEED	1/3 CUP RAW ORGANIC AGAVE
1 TBSP CHIA SEED	1-3 TBSP WATER, START WITH ONE
1 TBSP FLAX SEED	
2 TBSP RASPBERRY POWDER (OPTIONAL)	
24 NUTS OF YOUR CHOICE FOR TOPPING	
WALNUTS, MACADAMIA, PECAN, HAZELNUT	

Directions

1. Grind the 3 seeds together into a powder. If you don't have all 3 pick one or two and do 3 TBSP of any mixture of seed.
2. Mix all ingredients well in one bowl.
3. Put in refrigerator for 15-20 min.
4. Take a spoonful and make into balls.
5. Place nut of your choice on top.

Raw Food Energy Bar

SUGAR FREE, VEGAN, RAW FOOD

These bars are great to take when traveling, hiking or on your favorite outing. They help keep your energy level up with lots of protein and the blood sugar level even.

Serves 10-12 » Prep Time » 15 minutes » Dehydrate Time 10-12 hrs

Ingredients

2 CUPS RAW CASHEWS, ALMONDS OR WALNUTS

½ CUP SUNFLOWER SEEDS RAW

½ CUP RAW BLUE AGAVE

½ CUP FLAX SEEDS

3 TBSP RASPBERRY POWDER (OPTIONAL)

¼ CUP RAW ALKALINE CACAO

1 CUP MEDJOOL DATES PITTED

Directions

1. Soak Nuts and sunflower seeds in water for 1 hour; soak flax seeds in water for 30 min. Strain water.
2. Remove pits from Dates and mash very well into a paste.
3. In blender or food processor, put nuts, seeds, date paste and agave and puree.
4. Add Cacao and Raspberry powder, mix well again.
5. Spread evenly on dehydrator tray and dry for 10-12 hours.

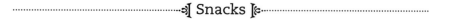

Ye Ol' Trail Mix

SUGAR FREE, VEGAN, RAW FOOD OPTION

Ahh…Trail mix! This is one of my favorite quick treats. Its quick and easy to make and great for grab and go. Great for road trips and yes of course…hiking the trails. It gives you the complete protein and carbs you need to keep the brain alert and the energy flowing. I love keeping this one raw, its better for the body especially the digestion, but sometimes it's hard to find all the raw ingredients unless you prepare them yourself. So at least try to keep the nuts and seeds raw.

Makes 8 Servings » Prep Time 10 minutes » Cook Time None

Ingredients

1 CUP RAW ALMONDS

1 CUP WALNUTS

1 CUP MIX AND MATCH OF RAW CASHEWS, MACADAMIA, PECANS, HAZELNUT, BRAZIL NUT OR PEANUTS

1 CUP RAW SUNFLOWER SEEDS

½ RAW GREEN PUMPKIN SEEDS

1 CUP RAISINS

½ CUP DRIED CHERRIES

1 CUP DRIED APRICOTS

½ CUP DRIED PINEAPPLE

1 DARK RAW CACAO CHOCOLATE BAR CHOPPED, 1 CUP OF NIBS OR CAROB CHIPS (OPTIONAL)

Directions

1.   Put in Large Bowl, mix well. Store in airtight Ziploc..Keeps for months!

Index

Index

Made in the USA
Charleston, SC
22 January 2014